Training Salesmen on the Job

Second Edition

To Prim and Susan

Training Salesmen on the Job

Second Edition

JOHN LIDSTONE

Gower

First published 1975 by Gower Press Limited
Reprinted 1977, 1978 (twice), 1979, 1981

Second edition published by
Gower Publishing Company Limited,
Gower House,
Croft Road,
Aldershot,
Hants GU11 3HR,
England

British Library Cataloguing in Publication Data
Lidstone, John
    Training salesmen on the job — 2nd ed.
    1. Sales personnel — In-service training
    I. Title
    658.3'1245   HF5438.2

ISBN 0 – 566 – 02414 – 4

Printed and bound in Great Britain at The University Press, Cambridge

Contents

Part Two – Techniques and Methods of Evaluation

List of Figures

Preface

The world in which sales managers and their sales forces operate has changed dramatically since *Training Salesmen on the Job* was first published ten years ago.

In the wake of recurrent energy crises, raw materials shortages, volatile international currencies and world-wide recession, companies have had to reshape themselves in order to survive, let alone prosper in markets that have stagnated or all but disappeared.

To provide the resources needed to compete internationally, companies have merged, becoming larger in size but fewer in number. In many markets, these large companies employ fewer but far more highly trained and skilled salesmen capable of selling to more professional, more demanding, more skilful buyers.

Rapid advances in computer technology have enabled most routine activities such as enquiry handling, order taking, processing and recording to be automated where once they were part of the salesman's responsibilities. Paradoxically this has released more time for the sales manager to man manage and for the salesman to sell.

Successive governments have created a plethora of laws influencing every facet of business life from employment, equal job opportunities and race and sex discrimination, to consumer protection and pricing controls.

Ranged alongside all these factors, the high cost of keeping a salesperson on the road has led company managements to ask themselves the question, 'what cost-effective role does the sales force play in achieving the company's marketing objectives?' Behind this question is the unspoken one, 'if we did not have a sales force, would we have ever invented one?'

For most companies the answer has been to recognise three stark facts of economic life.

- First, a sales force is an expensive marketing tool that must be directed selectively towards very specific objectives, markets and customers.
- Second, salespeople must produce profitable not just voluminous results to justify the financial investment.

● Third, in the fight for markets and for sales revenues, the role of the sales force is of crucial importance.

These economic realities are forcing companies to concentrate on the essential training and development needs of their salesmen.

Throughout the world thousands of men and women are employed in selling products, services or ideas. Some have been trained in the art of selling. Far too many have not. Yet in the highly competitive environment in which the majority of firms have to sell their products today, salespeople are often the spearhead of a company's total marketing efforts. They carry the main responsibility for getting through to the customer and securing the order. Vast financial resources are committed by commercial enterprises on the assumption that they will succeed in doing so.

As the managing director of a major manufacturer, summing up the challenge facing his company at the end of a national sales conference, said: 'after our clever marketing men and women have put their plans to bed, after production has made what our marketing researchers have told us people want and will buy, we are not in business until you (the salesmen) have sold these products *again* and *again* and *again* to our existing customers and to new ones. *That is the importance of the sales force.'*

Many firms recognise this and give their newly recruited sales personnel product training and sometimes sales training. But it is the continuous follow-up dedicated on-the-job sales training which maintains the selling skill in this highly competitive world that is still more conspicuous by its absence in the majority of companies.

Selling, a developed social skill upon which so much employment and prosperity depends, can and does fluctuate violently in quality and effectiveness and therefore in the tangible results it produces. When it falls below the level of competence required to meet the modern challenge, the cost in lost sales and morale is enormous. This variation in selling technique, I have observed and studied in nearly every country throughout the world over the last twenty-five years and have developed concepts and methods by which companies can ensure that their sales forces are selling effectively.

The training and development of the sales force on a day-to-day basis should be – as it has always been in the most successful companies – the key task of first-line sales managers. This can only come about by making sure that the managers who are responsible for the day-to-day activities of their salesmen are competent in two vital areas. First, that they are competent salespeople themselves and understand the nature of salesmanship. One of the ironies for most field sales managers is that, while they have to maintain the selling skills of their salesmen, it is probably many years since they were themselves *trained in selling techniques!*

Second, that *they are themselves trained to train* and so can impart knowledge of how to sell and develop this skill in other people. All too few field sales managers have had such training. It is therefore not too surprising that star salesmen and women are still promoted into management and *go on selling* instead of training others, and fail. And while many books on sales management highlight the importance of field sales training there has been a dearth of practical guidance on *how* to do it. It was that gap that inspired me to write *Training Salesmen on the Job* in the first place.

Although equal job opportunities have increased the employment of women in a wide range of selling and sales management jobs, the English language has not yet found an elegant way of expressing 'he or she'. Whilst I have changed some references in the text in this edition, please accept that when the terms 'salesman', 'man' and 'field sales managers' are used they apply with equal force to women as to men.

Purpose of this book

The purpose of this book is to provide a practical, tried and tested system and techniques for sales managers who are responsible directly for the on-the-job training and development of the sales force. It shows how new salesmen should be initially trained on the job and how to continue the individual development of experienced salesmen; how to appraise sales performance on the job and how to measure the effectiveness of such training. To many sales managers the ideas and techniques presented in this book will already be familiar. They have been applied, developed and used in America, the United Kingdom, in Europe and throughout the world, from Brussels to Bali. They are being used by companies with measurable success in a wide variety of markets from those selling capital goods, food and fast moving consumer products, pharmaceuticals, industrial and hospital products, to services such as advertising, banking, management consultancy, finance and accountancy, the law and architecture, broadcasting and government agencies.

Who should read this book

The book is written primarily for the sales manager who is directly responsible for the achievement of planned sales results through one or more sales staff. In particular, it is for managers who spend the bulk of their time in the field developing a team of salesmen, and in some sales forces, saleswomen. They may have the title sales manager, regional manager, district sales manager, area or country manager. To simplify, as well as identify their role, throughout the book I have used the title 'field sales manager'.

Contents

The book has been written and designed as a workbook for use by the field sales manager and the training manager and has been divided into two parts. Part One examines the market place in which the salesman operates and the nature of salesmanship, what the field sales manager aims to achieve through on-the-job training for the customer, the salesman and the company, and how the salesman should conduct the sales interview; each stage is reviewed in detail and diagnostically: exactly what to look for.

These four chapters remind the manager particularly of the skills in which he must be proficient and which he will aim to develop in his salesmen.

Part Two concentrates on the techniques and methods of evaluation: it describes in detail how to appraise salesmen on the job providing examples of appraisal formats; how to identify individual sales training needs; how people learn and communicate with each other and then how to train new and experienced salesmen.

In this second edition I have added new chapters and much new material. When accompanying a salesman, the field sales manager is involved in a wide variety of customer calls and must know how to adapt to each one. These are analysed and guidance given, in Chapter 9 'The Accompanied Call in Field Sales Management'. I have also written a chapter describing how to conduct successful sales training meetings. This provides guidelines on a group training meeting when a common weakness in the team indicates that this may be a more speedy and effective solution than the time it would take to train each salesman on an individual basis.

In the chapter on appraising selling performance, thanks to the willingness of a number of companies, I have been able to include examples of a variety of different appraisal systems currently in use.

How it should be used

Since this book concentrates on training salesmen on the job they do, it should spend most of its working life as a ready source of reference with the manager in his car. He should write against appropriate sections his own experiences and results in applying the techniques in the book. Checklists at the end of each chapter are designed so that managers can assess what is and is not being applied of the methods and techniques described in the book and what actions need to be taken.

The material in this book can provide the basis for a programme to train and develop the field sales manager as a trainer. This is the subject of my final chapter. Thanks to Peter Ross and his colleagues at Rank Aldis, a training film was made based on this book. Titled, 'Training Salesmen on the Job; training the experienced salesman' the film enables managers to see how to apply and use the Ten Steps in Field Sales Training.

Conclusion

In the widely acclaimed biography of Montgomery, *Monty The Making of a General* by Nigel Hamilton, the author spells out Monty's creed: 'The underlying principle of all training is the instruction of the leaders before they in turn teach their men'.

Training sales forces to sell successfully is like training soldiers to win a war. But instead of fighting with bullets, salesmen fight with products and customer benefits, triggered by customers' needs. But salesmen can only win their war if their managers have been trained to train them to win. It is with that always in mind that I have written this second edition.

John Lidstone

Acknowledgements

During the last twenty years I have had the rare opportunity to work with many hundreds of clients and managers in nearly every major country throughout the world helping them to implement the techniques described in this workbook. In addition, a large number of the thousands of managers who have attended workshops and seminars on management training have been kind enough to send me letters, reports and assessments of their successes and problems and how they tackled them. The numbers involved are so great that it is impossible to express individually my thanks and gratitude.

However, I would like to say 'thank you' to the managements of BOC Ohmeda, The George-Good Corporation, Kalamazoo, Pandair, Smith, Kline & French and Waverley Vintners for allowing me to reproduce examples of their sales force appraisal systems.

To Peter Ross and his colleagues at Rank Aldis for making a training film of this book and in doing so enabling the techniques of training to reach audiences in all parts of the world I would like to express my appreciation.

The concepts and techniques presented in the book have been the subject of continual evaluation by my colleagues at Marketing Improvements and I am grateful for the valuable comments and criticisms they have provided from working with our clients in nearly every type of industry and service.

JL

Part One

The Objectives of Field Training

1: Selling within the Marketing Environment

WHY DO WE NEED SALESPEOPLE?

Salesmanship, the art of persuading people to buy products, services or ideas is as old as the history of mankind. What is constantly changing is the market place in which salespeople and the companies employing them operate. Selling is like art. It mirrors the age in which it is practised. Historically, salesmen were employed to sell the products or services that companies decided to supply. This production-minded approach was only successful while the entrepreneurs who created them did not have too many competitors or, whilst products were in short supply, their salesmen could almost push goods on to customers or were persuasive enough to influence them to buy what the manufacturers had made.

Today this is no longer true. The development of the *marketing concept* has produced the greatest and most marked change in the attitudes of manufacturers and those who sell their wares to their greatest assets – their customers and potential customers. Most of the products and services we need have become plentiful, supply often outstripping the demand for them. Competition has not only become acute and ruthless between companies but has intensified between countries such as those in the European Economic Community, Japan, others in the Third World and America.

The secret of survival – let alone of success – in business has turned from the manufacture of products as such to the prediction of what people need and will want to buy.

Thus the development of the marketing concept – the creation of customers and keeping them satisfied – has led to the need to find out what people want and then make it rather than the traditional approach of making things and then trying to sell them. This approach, by no means new, recognises that customers create a business and satisfied ones are the cornerstones of its continued existence.

But the development of this customer-facing attitude and policy, however rigorously and imaginatively pursued, does not alone answer the problem of how to survive. What one company decides to do can also be done by others. The knowledge, skills and information among competing manufacturers large and small today are similar. What one company spends millions of pounds or dollars on over several years and invents today, others can imitate tomorrow. And patent laws, as the British pharmaceutical industry, song recording and film studios and makers of pocket calculators and other electronics goods have discovered to their cost, are no insurance against the pirating of their products. So another fact of commercial life has had to be recognised. That imitation is quicker and cheaper than invention and less risky. Similarly, the costs companies incur producing and distributing their products and services tend to be identical as are their ultimate selling prices to the buyer.

THE MARKETING ENVIRONMENT

The environment in which manufacturers, commercial, industrial and services companies operate and compete with each other is characterised by three factors:

Similarity of products and services

The products and services offered by competing companies tend to be similar if not frequently identical in appearance and advantages. Indeed in many of the fast moving consumer products such as foods and paper tissues, brand leaders stare across at themselves from opposite shelves in supermarket and self-service shops, except their twins are called 'own label' and are virtually the same product. There is little to choose between similar makes of mass-produced motor cars. In the electrical gadgets field the only difference between transistor radios, pocket calculators and tape recorders in similar price brackets is the manufacturer's name. Take the back off and all share a common origin – Japan or another far eastern source of cheaply produced printed circuitry. The catalogue of identical products is endless. Services such as banking and packaged holidays reflect the same pattern of similarity.

Similarity in prices and discounts

The prices charged by companies for similar products and services also tend to be alike. New and/or superior products and services are charged at a premium. This happy state of affairs lasts until a competitor enters the same market and starts to encroach on sales. Then prices are reduced. Thus with some very notable exceptions, in the vast majority of products and services we buy (detergents, petrol, food, clothes, banking and insurance) those offered by competing companies tend to be alike in product and service benefits and in prices we pay or discounts we are allowed if we are the distributor. And this is true whether we are marketing in London or Lisbon, in Scunthorpe or Singapore, since multinational companies develop transnational specifications for their products and parity of standards.

Presentation to the customer

The main difference between competing manufacturers, servicing companies, supermarket chains and multiple stores is in the way they communicate with their customers. It is the one area of the company's three things offered (products, prices, presentation) where the greatest control and direct influence can be brought to bear; in the *presentation* of products, services and ideas to the customer or consumer by means of public relations, advertising, packaging, direct mail, telephone selling, exhibitions and the sales force. But however good all the other methods of communication are, in the majority of companies the bulk of the presentational effort is carried out by the sales force (see Figure 1.1).

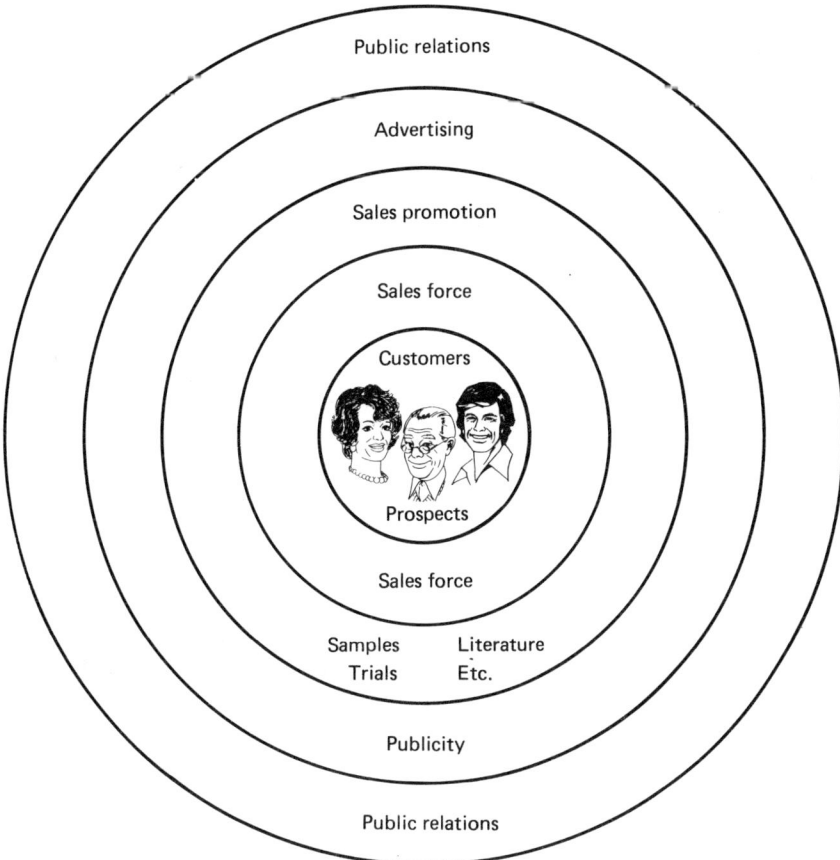

Figure 1.1 Circles of influence

The importance of the sales force becomes self-evident when you consider that in some markets the only difference between competing companies is the relative quality of their sales forces. In markets such as office equipment and life assurance, the buyer's decision is more often than not determined by who calls on him, what he says and how he says it. In many markets, the sales force is the only significant advantage a company has over its competitors.

THE CHANGING NATURE OF SELLING

There are other changes taking place that affect the role and the importance of the sales force. Six major changes can be seen.

1 The development of the market concept

During the 1960s, companies developed marketing departments which almost to the exclusion of other people, had the responsibility of 'looking at our business through the consumer's eyes and providing products and services to satisfy their needs at a profit'. Now we are passing through a stage in which such a concept not only involves the whole firm but all *functions* worry and give priority to the needs of the customer. But moving on again, prodded by an articulate and increasingly sceptical public, towards broadening the marketing concept, everyone in a business enterprise and not least the sales force is going to worry more about the *well being* of the customer, rather than just whether our products satisfy his needs – which marketing research has hitherto neatly identified.

2 The growth of multinational companies

The European Economic Community has changed the approach of many capital goods' producers, chemical manufacturers and retail stores towards their markets. A market or sales territory covering three or four countries rather than counties or cantons has become a common feature for many companies.

3 Companies are tending to become larger but less numerous

Takeovers and mergers bear ample and almost daily testimony to this development. Before 1939 there were over forty car manufacturers in the United Kingdom. Today there are at present only four major ones. At the beginning of this century every town of any size boasted its own brewery; today there are only ninety-nine in existence and this number is decreasing yearly. Such a development means that no company and, in particular, no salesman can let down such organisations in its product quality or in its service and hope to retain the business. For the salesman whose job is to develop and maintain business with such giant organisations, the implications are stark. The attitude of 'I was just passing by so I thought I would pop in to see if there was any business' is thankfully rarely heard by customers when salesmen call on them. But no less dangerous now is the attitude of salesmen to a call that failed in its objective either through lack of planning, seeing the wrong buyer or discussing the wrong product to meet a particular customer requirement: 'Oh well you can't win them all. I will get the order the next time round.' There will *not* be a next time for salespeople who have not done their homework before they call on customers. This is true of more and more marketing situations.

For example, two independent breweries were both taken over by a major hotel group. At that time there were three independent buyers upon whom the salesmen of products and services could call and sell. There is now either one buyer or one buying committee. This committee will not give a second interview to any salesman who has neither studied their needs nor has the relevant solutions to meet and satisfy them in product quality, price and follow-up service.

In the pharmaceutical industry in 1972 where medical representatives used to be able to see and present their products on a quarterly call to over 85 per cent of the 20 500 doctors in general practice, today 48 per cent of general practitioners will only grant two calls a year and then on an appointment basis; only 14 per cent of general practitioners will grant quarterly calls, and no less than 30 per cent of doctors will only see a medical representative once a year.

4 Buyers are becoming increasingly powerful

Flowing from the previous factor, the buyers of your products and services in the companies, manufacturers and retail shops/chains to whom your salesmen have to sell are, because of their purchasing power and the size of their orders, becoming much more powerful. Matching this increased power and influence they are also becoming much more sophisticated in their knowledge of the products of their suppliers; in financial knowledge and the effect on profitability of their buying; in negotiating the purchase of supplies, and furthermore in their own marketing and selling. A Swiss chemical company, an electronics group and one of the world's largest car manufacturers have taken the education of their purchasing officers to the point where they are given selling courses alongside their company's own sales force so they have a better appreciation of the selling techniques used by salesmen who call on them.

5 Competition

Competition between these giant organisations is increasing as each seeks to defend or expand market shares and control the key factors that influence prices and buyers' decisions. For example, manufacturers of motor cars, tyres, and car accessories own or virtually control their distributor outlets. Likewise, agricultural feed and fertiliser manufacturers are taking over merchant outlets. Every company, particularly multinationals competing with home based companies, is going to exploit every opportunity to expand at the expense of others.

6 Low growth conditions

In many sectors of manufacturing and service industries, national and international competitors are fighting to survive in conditions of low growth and in many countries, with stagnant markets coupled with more demanding, discerning critical customers.

THE ROLE OF THE SALESMAN

These factors of economic life and changes in the marketing environment do not lessen the importance of the sales force. On the contrary they mean that the sales force will have a more decisive influence on the success of marketing plans as their work becomes more specific. Companies have recognised that customers create a business, but only by keeping them satisfied can a company prosper. If they don't, others will. This means that every sales force must be recruited and selected, trained, motivated and developed to perform as skilfully as it can its prime and vital task – the reason for its existence – to identify the needs of customers and satisfy them.

Customers are becoming more sophisticated in their tastes, more knowledgeable about the products and services they buy or reject, and more critical and conscious of those who supply them. The salesmen who sell them must be more professional.

CONCLUSION

The marketing environment in which companies operate implies that salespeople will be needed as *never* before to perform a vital but changing function. Where once the salesman was a jack of all trades selling everything to everyone, he must now specialise, performing fewer tasks but more effectively and efficiently. Some companies are appointing salespeople to deal with just one major customer or to look after a particular sector of a market. The sales force and each member of it will be the spearhead and apex of a triangle through which more costly and tailored resources will flow.

New products, new technology and new techniques, mean that the salespeople must be creative in their selling rather than just react to customers and their needs. People's needs do not change, but the means of satisfying them do. However large companies become, they will ultimately succeed or fail, like the corner shop by their abilities to identify, anticipate and satisfy customers' requirements profitably. Likewise salespeople must be trained, motivated and controlled in such a way that they become more skilled in identifying and satisfying customers' needs faithfully, efficiently and constantly. Advertising cannot do this very effectively.

Computers cannot persuade computers. It is upon the quality of the sales force that the company ultimately depends for getting through to the customer and securing the orders that are necessary to achieve marketing objectives, planned profits and to survive.

For a great percentage of trading companies the linchpin of this success is the field sales manager. Upon him depends whether the sales force is *trained, developed* and *motivated* to succeed (Figure 1.2). The acceptance of this stark reality implies that whatever else sales managers are trained to do, *they must be trained to train their salespeople.*

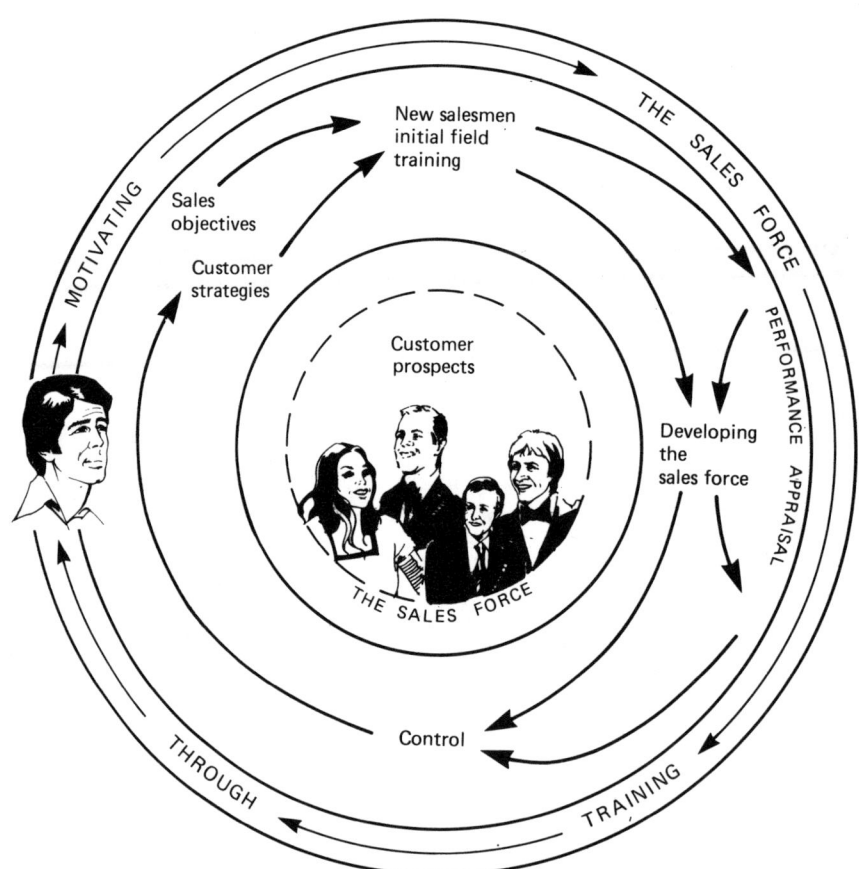

Figure 1.2 The field sales manager's job in the market place

Many of you will be familiar with the saying attributed to Bernard Shaw: 'He who can, does. He who cannot, teaches'. You may be tempted to agree with him. But like so many generalisations this one is rubbish. For if you accept that you are responsible for the training and development of your sales force then it follows that: *if you cannot train and teach, you cannot manage anyone.*

The principles, knowledge, methods and techniques the field sales manager can use to train himself to train and develop each of his salesmen on an individual basis, the young and the old, the new and the experienced, are presented in the following chapters.

Action planning checklist

	Answers	Action and timing
1 What changes are taking place in your markets served by the sales force in terms of: (a) Products? (b) Prices? (c) Presentation methods?		
2 What effect will these changes have on the sales force?		
3 What business-getting function will the sales force perform as a result of these changes?		
4 What actions and in what order need to be taken to ensure that the changed role of the sales force is: (a) Understood internally? (b) Effective in the market place?		

2: *The Field Sales Manager as Trainer*

The field sales manager is responsible for getting planned sales objectives achieved *through* the efforts of his salesmen and not *for* them. This means that the field sales manager must build and maintain a sales team which will be *stable, productive,* and *satisfied.*

DIFFICULTIES FACING THE FIELD SALES MANAGER

Getting planned sales results presents the field sales manager with certain difficulties which he must recognise and deal with if he is to be successful in obtaining them.

Initially he should recognise the fact that the salespeople he manages are normally *geographically spread.* They usually work from home and spend the greater part of their working lives in unsupervised situations. This causes problems of communication, motivation and control.

What should also be recognised is that *selling is a social skill* and salespeople are employed to use it to persuade customers to part with their own or their firm's money in exchange for products, services, or ideas. This is a socially unnatural situation and one which frequently brings customer and salesman into conflict, particularly those who sell consumer-durable products such as cars, double glazing, or encyclopedias, or intangibles such as advertising, insurance, etc. The things that are important to the customer are his needs, his problems and his requirements. Naturally, these are not as important from the salesman's point of view. He will tend to talk about his company, his products, and even the order he needs. As a result, salesmen are frequently rejected at the start of a sales interview or refused an order at the end of it. *This erodes their selling technique.* If salesmen are to be productive, sales training must be given as an essential and continuous process to repair morale and eroded technique.

Every field sales manager looks for that elusive gold mine 'the born salesperson' but few find him. There may be one or two star performers, but most sales forces are largely made up of average salesmen. Yet to combat resistance from customers and competition from other companies their selling must be *above average* to gain business. Sales training must be directed at creating the performance difference needed (see Figure 2.1).

DIFFICULTIES	IMPLICATIONS
1. Sales force – geographically spread	• Communicating • Motivating • Controlling
2. Selling – a developed social skill	• Keeping high standard of skill
3. Customers – often refuse salesman's proposition	• Loss of morale • Erosion of selling technique
4. Sales force unsupervised for over 90% of time	• Providing frequent leadership to repair morale • Training to develop selling skill

Figure 2.1 Four difficulties facing field sales managers

The field sales manager must recognise that those who choose selling as an occupation are usually the least equipped to cope with the strains that go with it. Selling attracts many men who have failed in their first choice of career either through lack of opportunity or of application to pass the necessary examinations. Such men often need constant, strong leadership, yet the very nature of the job makes it difficult to supply. Men who choose selling are usually very sociable individuals who enjoy and need constant companionship. Yet selling is socially one of the most lonely jobs a man can choose.

THE TRAINING FUNCTIONS OF THE FIELD SALES MANAGER

What then must the field sales manager do to get the sales results he needs through his sales team, bearing in mind that he will be judged by the sales he multiplies through them and not by the amount he sells for them? In order to build and maintain a stable, productive, and satisfied sales team and to overcome the difficulties that stand between him and this goal, the field sales manager must carry out four specific functions (see also Figure 2.2):

1 Train and develop new salesmen.
2 Train and develop experienced salesmen on a regular basis.
3 Appraise and evaluate the sales performance of his team so that necessary action can be taken to ensure achievement of planned sales objectives.
4 Motivate the salesmen to achieve their sales objectives.

In carrying out these four functions he will be providing the two ingredients essential to sales success: leadership and support for men faced with a lonely life and isolated from day-to-day contact with the company; and training to develop their skill and combat the constant wearing-down process caused by customer contact. Bear in mind that *if a manager cannot train, he cannot manage.*

Prime job objective: To achieve planned sales objectives through the efforts of his sales force

Key tasks	Knowledge	Skills
1 Train and develop new salesmen		
2 Train and develop experienced salesmen on a regular basis		
3 Appraise and evaluate sales performances of the sales force on an individual basis		
4 Motivate the sales force to achieve planned sales objectives		

Figure 2.2 The field sales manager's job

THE MAIN CAUSE OF FAILURE AMONG FIELD SALES MANAGERS

The manager can only be successful if he recognises that his role is that of a teacher not of a salesman. He must develop others to sell and not seek frequent opportunities to show off his own prowess as a salesman. This is the fundamental difference between being a salesman and managing salesmen. It is also one of the root causes of failure among field sales managers.

He is usually promoted because he has shown he is a good salesman. Yet as a field sales manager that is the one thing he must resist doing. If then he has not been trained to train others, what does he do?

Frequently he sees his job as getting out with his salesmen and involving himself in their sales calls. The better he is as a salesman, the more he will be tempted to take over the sales interview in the mistaken belief that somehow this will teach them how to sell. Rarely will it improve the selling skills of the salesman he accompanies.

THE FIELD SALES MANAGER MUST BE ABLE TO SELL

To be successful he does not need to be a brilliant salesman. Nevertheless, he should be a competent one. He must understand the principles of selling and how to apply them so that he can impart this knowledge to his salesmen. During the course of field training new salesmen, he must be able to show by example the standard of salesmanship he wants his salesmen to reach and exceed; only if his own standard is above average can he expect above-average performance from those who emulate him. And whilst he should not try and outshine his star salesmen, his own selling must command respect from the whole sales force to enable them to follow his leadership. Salesmen have scant respect for field sales managers who 'can easier teach twenty what were good to be done, than be one of the twenty to follow mine own teaching'.*

*The Merchant of Venice, Act 1, Scene 2.

CONCLUSION

The two major influences on any salesman are his customers and his field sales manager. Whilst his customers are the source of his sales and his success, the field sales manager is the linchpin in that relationship. He multiplies and improves the presentation of the company and its products through his salesmen. Through his skilful training he counteracts the erosion of selling technique which customers have on his salesmen. Through his training he leads and manages his salesmen towards the company's objectives and in doing so satisfies the needs of each salesman. *But if he cannot train he cannot do any of these things.*

3: The Nature of Salesmanship

Before examining the selling techniques the field sales manager will train his salespeople to use, the selling process first needs to be understood. Why, for example, do we need salespeople at all? Indeed, what is selling?

WHAT IS SELLING?

It is widely believed – and among many sales managers too – that selling has a mystique of its own and cannot be analysed. The dramatic rise of some of the washing-machine empires during the 1960s and the more recent growth of financial and unit trust operations have been attributed to the wizardry of born salesmen aided by occult powers. This mystery even remains when some of the most successful practitioners write books about selling, largely because they do not understand it and so cannot explain what they do and how they do it.

Although selling is different from all other business activities, it is possible to define and set out certain features which are common to all sales situations. It is then possible to say what basic requirements a person needs to become a salesman. Many field sales managers believe that if a person can sell, say, grocery products, they will be equally successful selling industrial products or intangibles such as insurance. Whilst every sales manager can quote success stories to prove this point, there are nevertheless dangers in taking this assumption (or wishful thinking) too far. Selling is not a unitary vocation in which people start at a certain basic level sales job and automatically graduate through stages to different and more complex types of sales activity. Paradoxically, many of the most difficult sales jobs are the easiest to obtain, for example, selling speciality products such as household hardware, life assurance, or encyclopedias. They have also been the graveyard of thousands of sales careers.

Nine distinct types of sales position can be classified, as shown in Figure 3.1. Most sales jobs are combinations of one or more of these categories, particularly those such as technical adviser

	Type of position	Sells	Job characteristics
1	Inside order taker	Usually serves behind a shop counter. Customers have made up their minds to buy, e.g. groceries, hardware. He serves them; he may suggest alternatives	Little opportunity for creative selling but may trade-up choice; main job requirements are to be reliable, of good appearance and courteous
2	Van salesman	Mainly delivers food and non-food products, e.g. fuel oil, coal, laundry, soft drinks, milk, bread, etc.	Reliability. A pleasant manner and good service are more important than aggressive selling. Few do any creative selling
3	Manufacturer's salesman calling on retail trade	Sells food and non-food products to shops, supermarkets, cash and carry, e.g. detergents, hardware, food, books, etc.	Mostly repeat selling; a pleasant manner, good service and reliable to follow a regular journey cycle; little scope for creative selling
4	Goodwill builder 'missionary salesman'	Educates potential users of the product or users to widen or increase their use of it, e.g. pharmaceutical products to doctors, brewery representatives, and specifier's products (architects, engineers)	Usually cannot take orders but builds a climate of awareness in which the benefits of a specific product or service will be favourably considered when the need arises
5	Technical salesman	Sells electronic equipment, industrial products or highly engineered component parts to original equipment manufacturers	Major emphasis is on technical know-how. Often too preoccupied with technical details: tends to forget the job is to sell. Far better to employ someone who can sell than an engineer who might or might not!
6	Creative speciality salesman of tangibles	Sells consumer durables that are often desirable but not essential, e.g. washing machines, cars and educational books	Has to make the prospective customer dissatisfied with the existing product or situation before he can begin to sell the product. This requires a highly structured selling presentation and he is a salesman who faces many refusals; a sales job often truly described as 'hard' selling
7	Creative speciality salesman of intangibles	Sells intangibles which are often desirable but not essential to life, e.g. advertising space, life assurance, stocks and shares, incentive schemes and banking services	Usually more difficult than the previous category because the product is less readily dramatised; its benefits come later or are difficult to comprehend. A very hard selling job requiring persistence and a highly structured approach
8	Political or indirect salesman	Sells products or services to large users:fuel-oil contracts, flour to bakeries, cement to local authorities, chemical aggregates such as sand, gravel, etc.	Usually little or no difference between competing products or services offered. The salesman only has himself to be better at looking after the needs of the buyer; he is a wheeler-dealer, sometimes a skilled negotiator, and sometimes a politician

Figure 3.1 The nine categories of sales position

Type of position	Sells	Job characteristics
9 Multiple salesman	Sells products or services to groups of people such as committees, boards of directors, project teams of engineers, e.g. computers, technological products for defence equipment, research or consulting services, pension schemes and merchant banking	The most difficult and skilled selling job; the salesperson usually makes presentations to several people with different, rather than similar needs. Usually more people say 'no' to his propositions than say 'yes'. He must have presence, charm and a highly-developed empathy

Notes

Categories 1 to 5 are usually highly structured in every aspect of the sales job, e.g. who to see or is seen, what to do and how to do it, the procedure for completing sales administration.

Categories 6 and 7 much less structured yet need to be to combat the high number of refusals which reduce the cutting edge of selling skill.

Categories 8 and 9 are only slightly structured. Also very few people are qualified to do this selling successfully. That is why they earn a lot of money as a rule.

Figure 3.1 The nine categories of sales position—*concluded*

or bank manager. A closer look at these categories, however, reveals an important distinction which must be taken into account when considering the training a particular type of salesman requires.

The differences relate to the extent to which each sales job is structured, e.g. how precisely every aspect of the sales job is defined, spelt out, journey cycled and supervised. As a generalisation, sales positions in the first five categories are highly structured; the next two far less so, while the last two categories have very little job structure.

A visit to a customer can be a mixture of many different situations: some simple ones of physical delivery, others involving high levelled and complicated negotiation. The man who can adapt to and gain business in such variable situations can be regarded as a professional salesman of the highest order.

WHY DO PEOPLE BUY THINGS?

It is easier to understand the true nature of salesmanship and define the basic requirements for a professional salesman if one first analyses the reasons why people buy, because in the nine categories of sales position there are basic needs common to all customers. The answer to the question 'what makes people buy?' is the cornerstone of salesmanship because it enables salespeople to plan how they can make themselves, their companies and their products or services interesting to each of their customers.

If we look at early 'primitive' society we find man took actions to satisfy his basic needs. The ultimate goal was simply to survive. To achieve this other needs, such as those for food, shelter, clothing and sex had to be satisfied. Nowadays these basic needs manifest themselves in many different ways. Nevertheless, whether at work (acting as a buyer for his firm) or at home (buying for himself and his family) people judge products, services, ideas and other people in the light of their own needs. We can state quite simply that: *people buy things and take actions to satisfy their needs.*

In most selling situations there are two people: a customer who has needs and a salesman who has products or services. Customers never buy the products or services a salesman offers but what the products or services do to satisfy their needs. These end results or benefits are the links in the chain that leads to a sale. When a salesman has no benefits to offer in the products he presents or in the language in which he describes them, then there is no sale. People will buy from a salesman and take the actions desired by the salesman if they know that by doing so they will receive benefits which will satisfy their needs.

WHAT ARE THE BASIC REQUIREMENTS OF A SALESPERSON?

The desire to satisfy particular needs is a characteristic common to anyone in a buying situation, whether they are the purchasing director of a major engineering group of companies or a pensioner. There are also certain characteristics which should be common to every salesperson. Like the nine categories of sales position, there will, of course, be big differences in their degree and emphasis, but the basic characteristics are the same. Two factors make these characteristics necessary. The first is that sales situations are for both the salesman and the customer unnatural social relationships. The second is that the things which are important to a customer are not always seen as important from the salesman's viewpoint, particularly if he has had little or no sales training. The result can, understandably, end up in the conflict of priorities shown in Figure 3.2.

Customer	Salesman
1 *Himself* Satisfaction of his needs, e.g. mortgage to buy a house, new machine to increase production	1 *Himself* His company His products His ideas
2 *His needs* and the benefits which satisfy them	2 *His product* and making this customer buy it
3 *This salesman* Salesman's company Salesman's products Salesman's ideas	3 *Benefits* to this customer
4 *Buying* from this salesman	4 *Customer's needs* Benefits which satisfy this customer's needs

Figure 3.2 Order of importance

The customer is most unlikely to see things from the salesman's point of view. *Everyone is to himself the most important person in the world.* Therefore to be successful the salesman has to be able to see things from the customer's point of view and demonstrate through his words and actions that he has done so. His chances of success are greater if he can understand the needs of the people he talks to and make them realise that he can help them fulfil these needs. The ability to do this depends on a combination of innate personality characteristics and acquired knowledge which can be summarised under four headings: The right job attitude, Product or service knowledge, Sales technique, and Work organisation.

The right job attitude

The salesperson needs to have a job attitude which combines the twin attributes of enthusiasm and empathy. Enthusiasm means wanting to establish himself, prove himself, be accepted by others and exercise control over the decisions made by others. Empathy involves the capacity for reacting to the experiences and emotions of others without necessarily taking their side; of wanting to help. To some extent these attributes cancel each other out, but the successful salesman combines the two in such a way that he meets the needs of the customer and achieves his own sales objectives.

Product or service knowledge

Product knowledge is too often taken for granted by companies and by salesmen. Sadly, experience of hearing countless hundreds of salesmen talking unintelligible gibberish does not support this complacency. Salesmen are usually given inadequate knowledge and it is slanted towards the company and not to the customer. Every salesman must be taught about products from the customer's point of view. This is a very difficult concept to grasp. Buyers buy to satisfy their needs. These needs are satisfied by the benefits of the product or service; these benefits are derived from technical features of the product or service. Salesmen should analyse everything they sell in this order before they meet a customer. In this way their thinking and their orientation will be towards the customer. No exercise repeated at regular intervals with each salesman will yield the field sales manager more sales than analysing products in terms of

Customer's needs ⟶ *Customer benefits* ⟶ *Product features*

Figure 3.3 illustrates how this is carried out.

Customer needs	Benefits that will satisfy customer needs	Product features from which the benefits are derived
1 *Rational* *Performance* – must be able to work fast with a variety of implements	Plenty of power, particularly at low speeds	A 65 BHP diesel engine with high torque at low r.p.m. Wide range of matched implements available
Versatility – must cope with a variety of soil and cultivating conditions	Can travel at a wide variety of speeds	A 10-speed synchromesh gearbox—four wheel drive available for very difficult conditions
Simplicity – must be easy to operate	Simple and speedy implement changeover. Easy to drive	Quick-attach linkage with snap-on hydraulic couplings. Ergonomically placed levers and pedals
Low cost – must be economical to run	Low fuel consumption	Efficient engine design with improved braking and fuel injector system. Good power/weight ratio
Reliability – must be able to operate continuously and be serviced quickly	Well-proven design with all basic snags removed. Local dealer with 24 hour parts service	More than 10 000 units already in operation. Wide dealer network with factory-trained mechanics backed by computerised parts operation

2 *Emotional*

Security – (fear of making wrong decision)	Most popular tractor on the market – 10 000 farmers can't be wrong	Largest company in the industry with good reputation for reliability and value for money
Prestige – (desire to gain status in the eyes of others)	Chosen by those engaged in best agricultural practice	Favoured by agricultural colleges and large farmers

Notes

1 The product analysis should be completed from left to right. Only when the needs have been identified can the appropriate benefits and the relevant features be selected.

2 If the salesman works from right to left not only will he lose his buyer's interest as he talks about items which may not be of interest, but also he will have no basis for selecting which benefits to stress.

3 This example is not intended as a complete analysis. That can only be done with a specific buyer in mind as each person has an individual need pattern. Performance will be most important to one farmer, low cost to another.

4 It will be noted that some of the product features are so technical as to be almost meaningless to the layman. This is one of the greatest dangers for the industrial salesman. Unless he translates his trade jargon he will fail to achieve understanding and thus cannot be persuasive.

Figure 3.3 Product analysis (Agricultural tractor example)

Sales technique

Selling skill is too often viewed as a natural ability or talent rather than a technique that can be acquired. A successful salesman is one who has mastered the art of persuasive communication. Sales technique involves understanding people's logical and emotional reactions to a sales presentation.

Salespeople are frequently subject to refusals. There are always more people who say 'no' to a salesman than 'yes'. This tends to demoralise the salesman because he may feel this refusal of his product as a social rejection of himself. Selling technique consists of doing and saying those things which will reduce the risk of refusal and make it easier for the salesman to reach his sales objective.

How people buy	How to sell	
	Sales objective	Sales technique
1 I am important 2 Consider my needs	To explore and identify customer's needs	Opening the sales interview
3 How will your ideas help me? 4 What are the facts?	To select and present the benefits which satisfy the customer's needs	The sales presentation
5 What are the snags?	To prevent by anticipating snags likely to arise or handle objections raised so that the customer is satisfied with the answers	Handling sales objections
6 What shall I do? 7 I approve	To obtain a buying decision from the customer or a commitment to the proposition presented to him	Closing the sale

Figure 3.4 The buying sequence

Sales interviews should be prepared, not played by ear. Such preparation gives the salesman more control over the sales interview.

The sales interview is usually considered to pass through the stages of identifying customer needs, creating interest and desire for the benefits that are offered, overcoming or preventing objections, and closing the interview by getting a buying decision.

How sales technique is applied to the buying sequence through which every sale passes is illustrated in Figure 3.4.

Work organisation

Salesmen must develop good work habits and be organised to make the other basic requirements of good salesmanship as effective and productive as possible. This involves classifying customers and prospects, planning customer meetings in advance, analysing sales interviews afterwards to improve future meetings, journey planning to avoid wasting unnecessary time travelling, and reporting activities accurately and when required.

A DEFINITION OF SELLING

It is important for the field sales manager and his salesmen that both know what selling is and agree a common definition to concentrate their minds and inspire their efforts to put it to work.

The types of selling done in all nine categories is usually *personal*. Even when faced by a group of people, the salesman is selling to *individuals* each with their own particular needs, preferences and prejudices. Customers want to be assured that a salesman understands their needs and their point of view. The salesman can only achieve this if his communication with the customer is *two-way*. In the eyes of many customers there is little difference between the products and services offered by competing companies. They have to be *persuaded* that there are differences which will help them.

Drawing all these factors together enables a definition of selling to be made as follows:

Selling is personal individual persuasive two-way communication aimed at achieving planned sales objectives.

Action planning checklist

	Answers	Action and timing
1 What is the company's definition of selling? If there is none, write one.		
2 What category(ies) of sales positions (see Figure 3.1) are employed in the sales force?		
3 How are these different categories of sales position structured to ensure that the salesmen are: (a) Trained regularly? (b) Motivated? (c) Controlled?		
4 What actions have been taken to analyse products on a 'customers needs: customer benefits' features basis, (see Figure 3.3) to ensure that salesmen communicate with customers from a needs viewpoint? If no actions are taken, make the necessary decisions by writing them down now		

4: *Field Sales Training Structures*

Field sales managers are responsible for producing the volume and quality of business needed to meet the company's profit objectives. Their ability to do this depends on the combined results achieved by the sales team. They must therefore aim to maintain and develop the sales effectiveness of the sales force by field training. From what has been said about the nature of the sales job in Chapter 3, the training and development of the sales team presents a formidable and continuous challenge and a test of resourcefulness, patience and perseverance.

They must constantly remind themselves of five problems. First of all, that they have to rely for the sales results they need on salesmen whose day-to-day performance is infrequently observed (some examples of this infrequency are given in Chapter 11). Second, that customers can erode selling skill. The third problem, and one not often thought about, is that a salesman's natural tension at the start and fear of rejection at the end of each sales interview are encouraged by the nature of his work. Left to his own devices for too long, his sales interviews will speedily deteriorate into bland, inconclusive unproductive conversations. Fourth, that to overcome these difficulties a salesman needs to plan and structure his sales interview. Such a plan and structure will keep him directed towards the customer's point of view and tuned to his needs. Ironically, although it is an aid and not a straight-jacket, the fifth problem is that salesmen dislike planning and structure.

Only by accompanying each of the salesmen as frequently as possible in their work can the field sales manager accurately and effectively carry out the aims of field training which are:

1 To check each salesman's selling performance against the standards set.
2 Find out what his weaknesses are and the real reasons for them.
3 Get the salesman to recognise these weaknesses (if there are any).
4 Correct these weaknesses by carrying out individual training and coaching on the job.
5 Encourage and show how selling technique can be improved.
6 Measure the improvements which result.

All this must be done with a high degree of skill and in an atmosphere in which there is trust and not suspicion between the salesman and the manager. The salesman should welcome the manager's presence and be a willing partner in wanting to achieve the standards they both desire through training. Above all else the manager will want the salesman to be more skilled *after* the training has been given. The manager must therefore be skilled to ensure that the salesman learns quickly and willingly in the limited time he can devote to each of his salesmen.

The aims of field training serve to emphasise that the prime job of the field sales manager is as a *trainer* and *developer* of salesmen. In order to assess individual performance so that he knows where to concentrate his training and thus always be in control of his men and what they produce, the field sales manager needs to know the principles of good salesmanship. He must be able to train his men in their use at the point of sale for his benefit, for their benefit, and not least of all, for the benefit of the customer.

THE STRUCTURE OF THE SALES INTERVIEW

For simplicity the sales interview can be broken down into its component parts. This will help communication between managers and salespeople; it will also provide a logical basis for analysing individual performance and help to define the areas which need correction. The component parts of the sales interview are:

1 Preparation
2 Opening
3 Presentation
4 Objections handling
5 Closing

Objectives	Methods
1 Specific objective(s) of call is?	
2 Plan to see . . . . who has the need and authority to make a buying decision.	
3 My opening will be designed to	
4 My presentation will aim to	
5 I anticipate that the following objections will arise: (a) . . . . (b) . . . . (c) . . . . (d)	
6 I want to obtain the following decision(s) from the buyer: (a) . . . . (b)	
7 To support my sales presentation I need the following equipment, visual aids and correspondence:	

Figure 4.1 How sales interviews should be structured

This is the structure around which a salesman should build the flesh of his interviews so that the problems of tension, nervousness, lack of appeal to customer needs and woolly talk are reduced. An example of a structured format for planning a sales interview is illustrated in Figure 4.1.

The benefits of having a structure

Many salesmen and some managers discount the need for planning the sales interview. They will argue that because one cannot foresee what the customer will do or say, planning and preparation are pointless. This is making perfection the enemy of the good, because to some salesmen such preparation implies a muzzle on the mouth. But can a manager afford to have salesmen playing sales interviews off-the-cuff when the company's turnover depends on the way they communicate with customers, who are short of time, and when competitors are also after the business?

One of the most interesting traits of salesmen is that even those who have had no sales training tend to follow a structure for their sales interviews. A field sales manager can find this out by noting down the salient points of a series of sales interviews conducted by a salesman. The salesman develops a patter which tends to repeat itself call after call. This characteristic can be used by the manager as a basis for selling to the salesman the benefits of having a plan and a structure based upon the *customer's needs*.

Another factor he can mention to support the case for having a structure is that customers are not going to help the floundering salesman to sell them what he wants. Thus selling technique skilfully structured provides stepping stones that bring him and the customers to the point of purchase. This is illustrated in Figure 4.2.

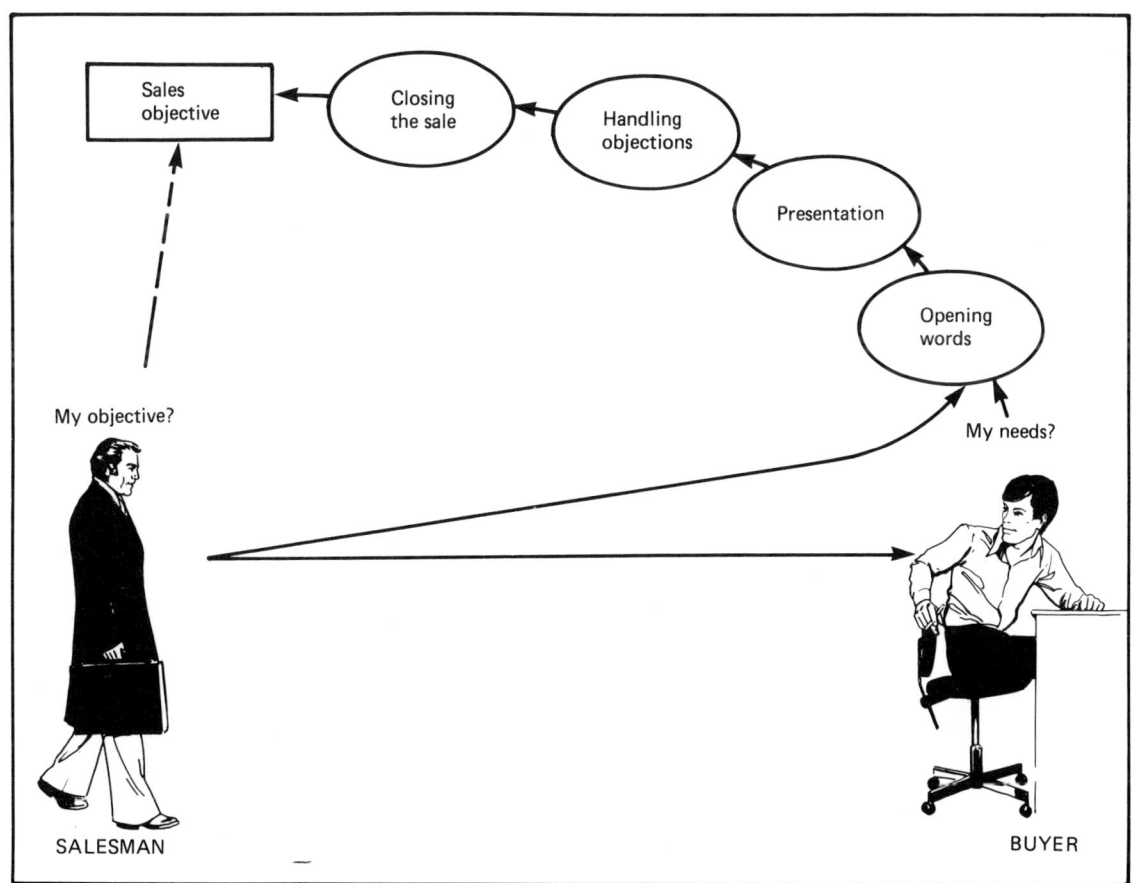

Figure 4.2 Stepping stones to sales objectives

Preparation

The cornerstone of preparation is the proper use of customer records. Too few salesmen regard such records as an aid to their selling, more as a chore that head office insists they maintain. The benefits to the salesman of an effective record system will be the information it provides about the needs, habits, idiosyncracies of customers and prospects, the numbers and types of decision makers in a business who can influence the sale, the products they use and don't use, and why, and a host of other data. Customer records will help the salesman to identify the *correct* objectives for a sales interview and enable him to plan how best to achieve them. The benefits of preparation can be summarised as follows:

1   It gives the salesman confidence because he knows what he plans to do and how he is going to do it.
2   It makes him think ahead. He knows in advance the broad lines of his plan, so that when carrying it out he can concentrate on listening to the customer and not become preoccupied with what to say next.
3   It enables him to talk in a positive way and from the customer's point of view.
4   It gets more business in the limited time there is available for selling.

What should the salesman prepare?

A salesman should think about the following factors when preparing each sales interview. The field sales manager, when observing a day's calls, can then tell whether they have been planned and, if so, how well.

Call objective(s) Is it clear that the salesman has a definite purpose for the call which will promote the sale of the company's products or services? If not why is he calling? General statements such as 'to sell our range of equipment' is not good enough or precisely defined. It fails to identify the customer and his individual requirements. The more specifically an objective is stated the greater the likelihood of success, for example: 'To reduce this customer's loss of production time by getting him to install our XJ1 Mechanical Handler.'

Opening words After the usual introductory courtesies, how is he going to get down to the purpose of his call so that the customer is made to think and talk about his needs or problems?

Presentation What benefits will he offer? Will they meet this particular customer's needs? What evidence will he use to prove the benefits he offers, for example third party reference success stories? What visual aids can he use to illustrate his story? Has he brought them with him?

Objections handling What objections is the customer likely to raise? How will he answer them?

Closing How is he going to close the interview and get a buying decision or commitment? Does it match his call objective?

If the salesman does all these things consistently then he is doing a good job for his field sales manager. If not, he is falling short of his potential and both he and his manager are the losers.

HOW SUCCESSFUL SALES INTERVIEWS SHOULD BE CONDUCTED

Whilst the preparation provides a call strategy, how is that plan to be implemented to achieve a successful sales interview? The field sales manager will have to watch and listen as the sales interviews unfold.

Opening

First impressions can be crucial. The unnaturalness of the sales situation sets up tension for the salesman and the customer. Planning will help to put the salesman at ease. His opening should put the customer at ease also, and do much more. At the start of the sales interview the salesman wants to achieve four objectives:

1 Create a good impression.
2 Gain the customer's individual attention.
3 Explore the customer's needs.
4 Get the customer talking about them.

Let us examine each of these objectives in turn:

Creating a good impression

Watch the salesman's mannerisms, his dress, his stance. Does he say and do those things which create a warm, friendly atmosphere which makes the business part of the interview run as smoothly as possible? Does he command respect? Is he polite without being servile?

Gaining the customer's attention

Does he make the customer listen because he wants to and not because he has to?

Exploring customer's needs

This is one of the most vital stages of the interview. Before any real communication can proceed, the customer must be given the time, opportunity and reasons to express himself. This can best be done by asking carefully directed but open-ended questions which get him talking rather than making monosyllabic 'yes' or 'no' replies.

The questions chosen and the words used will dictate the area of need the salesman wants to concentrate on or explore. If the questions begin with: How? What? Where? When? Who? Why? Which? then they will invite and encourage comment from the customer. Such questions should allow comment and not require justification or defence.

An example of the open-ended questioning technique

A bank manager is anxious to obtain the account of the owner of a firm who he knows is planning to step up production dramatically and is going to need money to do it. The bank manager has been granted an interview with the managing director, whose account is held by another bank. The introductions have been made and the interview begins:

> *Managing director:* 'Do you know this is an unusual experience for me. I usually have to come and see my bank manager and not for the most agreeable of reasons. You must want something.'
> *Bank manager:* 'No Mr Head, the purpose of my visit is to find out whether I can help you. Let me explain. This report in last week's *Echo* about your proposed expansion plans (here manager opens newspaper and shows to Mr Head) was it correct?'
> *Managing director:* 'Yes except they did not say how much overseas business we hope to win.'
> *Bank manager:* 'That is most interesting. My congratulations. Tell me how much increased production do you plan?'
> *Managing director:* 'At least 25% by next December.'

25

Bank manager: 'How much will this cost?'
Managing director: 'Our first estimate is about £282,000
Bank manager: '*How* do you plan to raise that kind of finance?'
Managing director: 'I was wondering whether you might have some proposals that we could consider?'

As soon as the answers indicate an area of *need* which the salesman can meet and satisfy, he is in a position to sell benefits to the customer. The greatest single failing of salesmen is their inability to understand the concept of needs, discussed in Chapter 3, and their reluctance to identify them. Yet knowledge of and identification of each customer's needs are the prerequisite of all successful selling.

Presentation

If the salesman is successful in establishing a person's needs or identifying his problem, he is halfway to success. The customer will be interested but he wants to know whether the salesman's proposition will produce benefits which satisfy his needs or solve his problems. During the presentation the field sales manager must watch the customer and listen to what is said with great care, because it is during this meaty stage of the interview that the salesman falls into the trap of talking about product features.

Some examples of what salespeople say about their products or services which they fondly (and also foolishly) think will appeal to the customer now follow. All are true.

Example one
A valve salesman is selling plug-type valves containing a chemical, the benefit of which is that it keeps the valve permanently lubricated and therefore trouble free. He is talking to a sewerage works superintendent.

Salesman: 'And above all, the best thing about these valves is that they are low Mu.'

The result of the call was no sale.

Example two
A sausage salesman is selling a brand of sausages in a small shop which has just been bought by a married couple new to the retailing business. The sausages are pork and in packets of eight. The benefit, if there is one, is obscure:

Salesman: 'As you are wanting to start with a good balanced stock of popular sausages you will want some pork eights, won't you?'

The result of the call was no sale.

Example three
A salesman is selling corporate credit cards to the general sales manager of a company employing 10 export sales executives. He has worked out that if the general sales manager gives his salesmen credit cards the benefit to them will be the convenience of not having to carry considerable sums of money with them on each tour. But this is not a benefit as such to their manager.

Salesman: 'The great benefit to them, of course, and to you too, is that they need never carry large amounts of cash in future on their overseas visits. That must make it worthwhile mustn't it?'

General sales manager: 'It may be worthwhile to them but as it appears to offer me no tangible improvement on savings I think we will carry on as we are.'

Example four
A salesman is selling double glazing which he claims will save a householder at least £10 a week in heating costs. One housewife to whom he said, 'Wouldn't you like to save £10 a week off your heating bill surprised him by saying, 'No'. When asked, 'Why not?' she told him that she did not spend that amount each week on heating anyway. That was the end of the conversation. No benefits to the customer, no sale for the salesman.

Does the salesman think and talk about benefits?
Remember, benefits are the desirable results from the customer's point of view and, in business terms, from the points of view of all the other people the customer is concerned with – his customers, his staff, and their families. Benefits do not include any of the following:

1 The technical features of a product or proposition: 'This boiler has a thermal capacity of 85 000 BTUs.' 'This unit trust policy includes life cover.'
2 The way a product is packed.
3 The price of the product or service.
4 The methods of operation.

Benefits are the desirable results produced by these various features for any person who uses the product. Their effectiveness and their appeal depend on the extent to which they satisfy a customer's needs or problems. People buy products, services, and ideas, for what they *do,* not for what they are.

Does the salesman use third-party references?
In other words, does he make skilful use of the satisfaction experienced by other customers who have bought the product or service? In particular, does he focus upon the benefits they are getting? To prevent the choice of any third-party references backfiring on him, does he mention people or firms who: Are respected by the customer? Are faced with the same conditions?

Does he use stories to illustrate his argument?
Does he explain what other companies or customers have actually said about their experiences, either with or without his company's products?

Does the salesman ask progress test questions?
A productive sales interview involves two-way communication. It is important that the salesman gets feedback from the customer to confirm if he has heard, understood, and agreed so that any doubts can be cleared up and questions answered. Does the salesman during the presentation check these things by asking questions such as: 'Am I right in thinking this is what you want?' 'How does this strike you?' 'What would your family think about that?'

Does he use visual aids?
Models, catalogues and leaflets add variety to his presentation and pictures to his words. Does he: Keep visual aids hidden until needed? Stop talking when the customer is looking at them? Remove them after use to minimise distraction?

As a brief summary, check the presentation against these points. Does the salesman: Talk about benefits related to the customer's needs? Use third-party references? Use stories to illustrate his argument? Ask progress test questions? Use visual aids?

Objections handling

Sooner or later in the majority of sales interviews, objections will be raised. Obviously salesmen must know the answers. But knowing them and putting them across to the customer's satisfaction are two different things.

Winning an argument may satisfy the ego but is not very productive. How can field sales managers help their staff in this area? First, is the salesman aware of the existence of the raised emotions which accompany an objection and does he take steps to remove or reduce unfavourable emotions either by listening to the objection without interruption or by 'sparring'? By the latter is meant pausing after hearing the objection out, answering the customer by saying the objection is understandable and deserves serious consideration, and playing back the customer's question to clarify full understanding and to check if it is the only objection preventing the customer deciding to buy. The 'sparring' technique is illustrated in Figure 4.3. Having 'sparred' with the customer, does the salesman use the right methods to overcome the particular objections raised?

If the field sales manager finds that several salesmen are meeting the same objection he can help them by placing it on the agenda of the next sales meeting and setting aside time to work out satisfactory answers with them using actual customers' interview statements as case histories. (See Chapter 12, How to Conduct Successful Sales Training Meetings.)

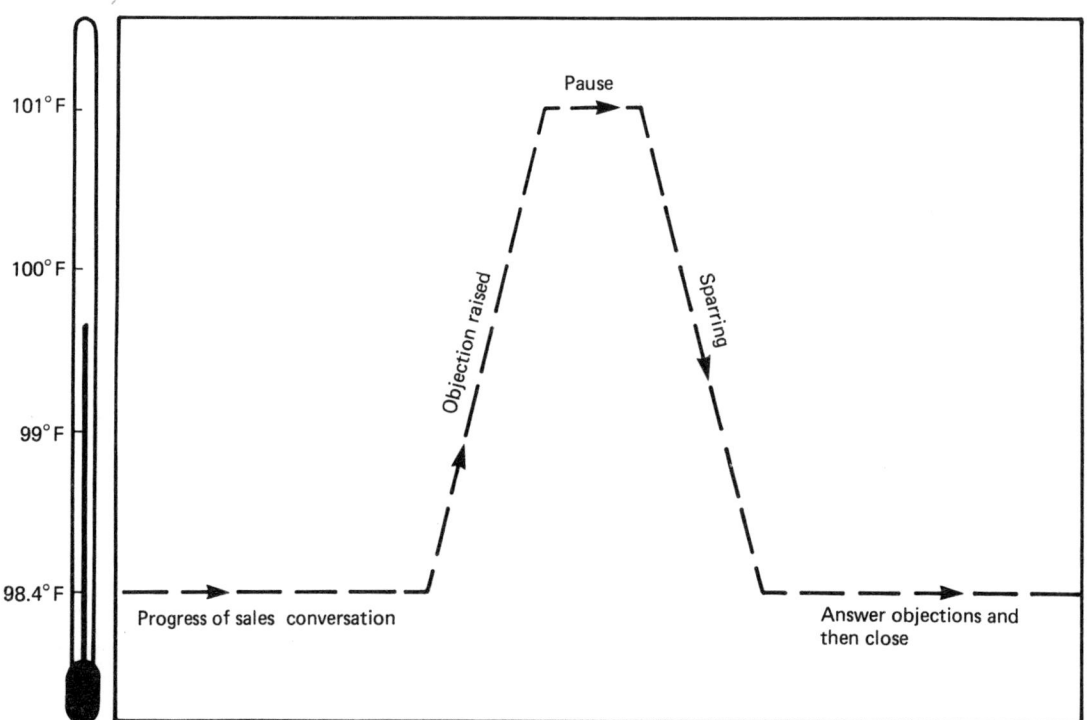

Figure 4.3 Sparring with objections

Closing

Closing the sale by asking for a buying decision is one of the weakest areas of sales techniques. It needs to be the strongest. There are two main problems.

The main problem is in the salesman's mind – his fear of social rejection. In a free society where customers can usually buy from at least two suppliers salesmen cannot escape rejection from time to time. Yet unless he closes the sale successfully, his chances of achieving his preset objectives are nil. Putting it bluntly: 'If you can't close you can't sell.'

The second problem is that salesmen believe the close is divorced from the actual progress of the sale and that the presentation will be sufficiently beguiling for the customer to buy without being asked. This rarely happens. The close only converts acceptance of the idea, plan or product into action. The close is also important for the customer. He needs this help to reassure him in the decision he wants to make or has made.

What is a close?

A close is the achievement of the preset objective of a salesman's call. In most industries it is the signing of the order. Some salesmen work in industries, particularly the goodwill builders – the category four people – where the nature of the trade makes it difficult to obtain the order physically at the end of the sales interview. Pharmaceutical representatives promoting ethical drugs to doctors, brewery representatives, manufacturers of building products promoting their products to architects, surveyors and town planners, etc, are examples of this.

Whatever the sales situation there are major indications that a customer has 'bought' and can be asked to commit himself in words. These indications include:

1   When he actually says he will buy the product or write it into the specification.
2   When he asks searching 'buying' questions about the in-use characteristics of a product: the type of service most relevant to his type of business; in the case of a doctor speaking to a pharmaceutical representative, questions about the dosage, side effects of a drug, etc.
3   When a customer names the product in the context of using it to solve a problem or getting it to solve someone else's need that he is concerned with.
4   When he asks if he can have a demonstration or a trial.

When to close

The close should be attempted by the salesman immediately acceptance of the idea is shown. This acceptance may be the customer's outright statement that he wants to order. More often his acceptance will manifest itself in the form of *buying signals* or buying questions such as questions about the success rates other people have achieved with the product, its side effects, in-use characteristics, or the method of payment; also discussions about the order size or guarantee period, etc. The tone of voice, hesitancy, posture, the calling in of another person to give an opinion or to have a look or admire, are also signals.

If the salesman has checked each step of his presentation to ensure understanding and agreement he is better able to judge the psychological moment of acceptance and to close.

How to close

At the close it is imperative that the salesman should concentrate on the customer and the satisfaction of his need or problem, and not on the product. There are many techniques for closing. The salesman must know how to employ them and which ones will be most effective in any given sales situation. The important point is that the salesman must close clearly, confidently and persuasively. His choice is very much dependent upon the type of persuasion needed with a particular customer. Here are the most widely used and most effective ones:

The direct request
'May I go ahead and place an order for two machines?'

Immediate gain from immediate decision
'By opening a deposit account immediately you can get the maximum benefit from present

interest rates now.'

Alternatives
'Which of these two models do you prefer, the green one or the white one?'

Assumption
'You have obviously already decided what to do. The only problem we have to deal with now is the quantity you are going to need to commence production next month, isn't it?'

Third party reference
'Bloggs and Partners, similar to yourselves, have invested in this system and have been able to reduce staff costs. Would it not benefit you to do the same?'

Summary close
'There are four benefits you can enjoy . . .' (then list them one by one keeping the most important to the end).

Closing on a question or objection
Doctor: 'What preparations do you offer?'
Salesman: not: '20 × 25 and 200 × 25 mg, or in suspension of 4 oz', *but:* 'How will you want to use it?'

After the close
The close is made when the objective of the sales interview has been achieved. If the salesman fails to do this, does he keep the initiative by mentioning or arranging another meeting? If he succeeds, does he give the customer a feeling that he has achieved something worthwhile and not been bested? Does he provide this reassurance by repeating the main benefits the customer will obtain from the decision he has made?

CONCLUSION

Field sales managers are the only managers who have to rely so heavily on staff who are geographically widely-spread. They also have to rely on the social skills of their men. It is a sobering thought that the survival of some of the largest corporations ultimately depends upon the persuasive tongues of a handful of people scattered throughout the country!

Dealing with a variety of individuals, subjected to unnatural social encounters, separated for long periods from their superiors, these salesmen can easily develop bad selling habits which can spoil their performance. The field sales manager carries the responsibility for ensuring that their selling time is used as profitably as it can be. Remember that few salesmen actually sell, that is expose themselves to the danger of getting business, for more than 20% of their working day. The tools of selling are the salesman's words and actions. He is in direct competition with salesmen from other companies. He uses words to gain business. His words can also lose business. The notes set out in this chapter provide guidelines which will help the field sales manager in the training and development of his salesmen's technique.

Action planning checklist

	Answers	Action and timing
1 Does the company have a definition of management? If not write one as it can apply and be understood by field sales management		
2 Does the company have an organised programme of field sales training for the whole sales force?		
3 Does the company have an organised programme of field sales training for all new salesmen joining the company? If not what actions need to be taken to design one, either by the training department or by an external body?		
4 Have the field sales management been trained in selling technique? If not, what actions need to be taken to ensure they are trained?		
5 Has the company a system for identifying objections met by the sales force and working out methods of answering them to the satisfaction of customers?		
6 Has the company developed methods of obtaining commitments from customers and trained the sales force in how and when to use them?		

Part Two
Techniques and Methods of Evaluation

5:

How to Appraise Selling Performance

If he is to get planned sales objectives achieved through the efforts of his salesmen, the field sales manager must know *how* they are performing as individuals and as a group. Sales figures, new account openings, orders-to-calls ratios, and a host of other statistical information, will tell him *what* each person and what the sales team as a whole have produced. They will not tell him *why* a particular salesman is succeeding or failing.

THE MANAGER'S NEED FOR AN APPRAISAL SYSTEM

To measure how well or badly each salesman is performing compared with the sales objectives they have been set, the manager needs an appraisal system which will help him find the answers to six questions:

1 What standards of performance are required of the salesman to achieve his budgeted sales targets?
2 What is his actual performance?
3 What are the differences between his performance and the standards set?
4 To what are the differences attributable: where are there deficiencies?
5 How can these deficiencies be eliminated?
6 What action plan should be agreed for the coming year?

Until the field sales manager has a clear and precise knowledge of what the salesman is doing correctly and what he is not – of his areas of weakness and his motivation and attitude, or the extent to which he lacks product knowledge, or whether his sales technique or work organisation is faulty – no remedial action can be taken. For him an appraisal system is essential.

THE SALESMAN'S NEED FOR AN APPRAISAL SYSTEM

By the same token, the individual salesman needs to know precisely what he is expected to accomplish. He needs some yardstick which he can apply to his own performance so that he can assess the quality and quantity of his sales work in relation to what he has to produce and is producing.

He needs a checklist or a set of guidelines to remind him on a regular basis of his principal activities and inform him of what is considered satisfactory performance. This is vital for those salesmen who, because of the nature of their sales work, do not get feedback in the shape of written orders at the end of each call, e.g. pharmaceutical salesmen and those who promote their products through architects and specifiers. For the salesman an appraisal system is also essential.

THE COMPANY'S NEED FOR AN APPRAISAL SYSTEM

The turnover and profits the company needs depend to a large extent upon the performance of the sales force. Thus the results the salespeople produce can be regarded as the company's yield from its investment in them. But to produce any increase in this yield the company needs to be sure that these human resources are growing and if this growth is retarded for any reason where and why is this so? For the company an appraisal system is essential.

Many companies have developed very comprehensive appraisal systems to enable decisions to be made fairly objectively about the development of staff for promotion: salary reviews and the nature and scale of departmental and individual training needs. There are a number of excellent guidelines on the design of appraisal systems the sources of which are given in the bibliography at the end of this book. This chapter shows how to appraise the salesman on-the-job. Some companies distinguish this type of appraisal from the annual or bi-annual one, by calling it 'Field' or even 'Call' Evaluation.

WHAT TO APPRAISE

The field sales manager should appraise the key factors which relate to the job the salesman should be carrying out. These will be concerned with what is done during the sales interview

Knowledge required of	Skills required: ability to
The company: its marketing policies and procedures	Organise personal work to optimise selling time
Delivery, routeing, credit and pricing policies, accounts collection, legal implications and servicing	Write reports
	Understand computer data and complete orders accurately
The markets in which he is selling; knowledge of customer's business operations	Analyse a sales territory, establish sales potential, and identify prospects
The products/services or ideas he is selling and those of his competitors	Prepare sales interviews
New products being introduced by the company and by competitors	Communicate fluently and persuasively
	Open sales interviews effectively
Old products being phased out by the company and competitors	Present a sales proposition based on customer needs
Selling done by others in the company, e.g. national accounts negotiators, inter-divisional selling, etc.	Deal with customer objections
	Use visual aids effectively
	Close the sale effectively and continuously
Reporting and complaints procedures	Deal with complaints
	Analyse own sales performance in order to improve

Figure 5.1 Basic data for content of salesman appraisal form

which directly influences the quantity and quality of the sales results produced. In order to sell effectively and efficiently a salesman must not only have appropriate job attitudes but also certain knowledge and skills.

The factors which influence his selling skill and the standards of performance he must reach and maintain will include some or all of those listed in Figure 5.1. Too many appraisal forms suffer from a surfeit of factors which have to be assessed. The appraisal form should list as few factors as are relevant to the job and essential to guide the manager and the salesman towards the answers they need to improve performance.

Generally speaking, such an appraisal should cover the following areas: product knowledge, selling technique, and sales administration.

CONTENT AND DESIGN OF A SALESMAN APPRAISAL FORM

Appraisal forms are not difficult to design but unless they reflect certain basic principles they will become a source of gripes rather than an instrument for the growth of knowledge and development of selling effectiveness. What are these principles?

1 The form should be totally acceptable to the men being appraised. Therefore:
   (a) The rating scales used should create as little emotional reaction as possible, so avoid terms such as 'very this' or 'very that'.
   (b) Concentrate on agreed standards that are derived from the techniques employed by the salesman.
   (c) Avoid the suggestion that 'achievement' indicates no training need. Even the best performances can be improved.
2 The form should concentrate on the present job being performed.
   (a) The manager and the salesman should use the form as a means of identifying and agreeing those areas of the salesman's performance which can and need to be improved to the benefit of both him and the company.
   (b) For this reason the form should concentrate on performance factors related to the present job and avoid any reference or rating about 'management development' or 'future potential.' These should be dealt with at the annual appraisal.
3 The form should be as concise as possible and clear in its format.
4 The form should be well designed and look important.
   (a) Avoid cramming too much into too little space.
   (b) Have the form professionally printed on good paper. This will enhance its importance. A duplicated form will diminish its importance.
   (c) Have it printed on coloured paper. This will make it easily identifiable.
   (d) Allow ample space for explanatory comments. Comments clarify needs and give the manager essential clues about the flavour of what happened in a particular situation. It also forces the appraiser to express his observations in his own words rather than taking the easy way out by just ticking a box.
5 The field appraisal, in contrast to the company's formal annual appraisal, should *not* attempt to cover too many factors of selling performance on any one occasion or field accompaniment.
   (a) select and agree the *known* and *relevant* factors
   (b) be very selective about introducing any additional factors
   (c) Remember that the factors pinpointed are those that you and the salesman agree are affecting selling performance and therefore need attention. You as the manager and trainer *must* be able to do something specific to improve those areas of selling performance selected.

Factors appraised	Customer calls made											Notes on calls made
	1	2	3	4	5	6	7	8	9	10	11	
Product knowledge												
Company												
Competitors												
Selling technique												
Call preparation												
Opening												
Presentation												
Use of visual aids												
Objections handling												
Closing												
Keeping initiative												
Work Organisation												
Customer appointments												
Customer records												
Call reports												
Accurate reports												
Care of equipment												
Care of literature												
Sales results												
Achieved call objective(s)												

Call Rating scales:

S = Satisfactory   AA = Above average   BA = Below average   U = Unsatisfactory

Figure 5.2 Salesman selling calls evaluation

Salesman . . . . Date of Call(s) . . . .

S = Satisfactory   AA = Above Average   BA = Below Average   U = Unsatisfactory

Factors marked X Appraised	S	A A	B A	U	Comments
Product knowledge					
Company					
Competitor					
Selling technique					
Preparation					
· Opening					
Sales presentation					
Objections handling					
Closing					
Keeping initiative					
Sales administration					
Work organisation					
Accurate reports					
Regular reports					
Customer record cards					
Care of company car					
Care of equipment					
Care of literature					

General comments
(Strengths, weaknesses)

Action taken

Recommendations
(training, self training, etc.)

Appraised by   *Salesman's signature*

Figure 5.3 Salesman performance appraisal

Two versions of a salesman (on the job) performance appraisal format are shown in Figures 5.2 and 5.3. Whilst the content is similar in both, they are used for different purposes. The main difference lies in the number of customer calls that can be appraised in the Figure 5.2.

This appraisal is designed to be used so that when accompanying a salesman for one or more days' work, a manager can record and evaluate a salesman's performance in a number of successive selling calls. The precise information accumulated provides a much more accurate foundation to pinpoint any sustained improvements from your last accompaniment or alternatively a weakness in a key technique such as call objectives or closing than would be revealed from observing just one or two selling calls. Moreover the total picture given by this appraisal will enable you and the salesman accompanied to review the strengths and weaknesses in each call and so arrive at an agreement as to precise training need to be tackled. In Figure 5.3 the appraisal form can be used at the end of a field accompaniment to summarise strengths and weaknesses, the actions you have both taken or are going to take in the future.

EXAMPLES OF SALESMAN PERFORMANCE APPRAISAL SYSTEMS

During the years since *Training Salesmen on the Job* was first published many hundreds of managers throughout the world have discussed with me their problems in designing practical and acceptable salesman Performance Appraisal Systems. Some of the systems in use are illustrated in Examples 5.1, 5.2, 5.3, 5.4, 5.5, 5.6, 5.7, and 5.8. I am indebted to the following companies for allowing these examples to be reproduced:

BOC Ohmeda
George-Good Corporation
Kalamazoo Business Systems
A major oil company
Pandair
Smith, Kline & French Laboratories Limited (United Kingdom Overseas Group)
Food, Drink and Tobacco Industry Training Board. This example is from a Van Sales Training Package produced when the Board was still operating.
Waverley Vintners Limited

PRODUCT COVERED Call evaluation form Before/after training	**BOC OHMEDA**					Date . . . . Salesman . . . . Customer . . . .

Selling activity	Yes No	Yes No	Yes No	Yes No	Yes No	Comments
1 *Pre-call planning* Did he have specific objective for call?						
Did he prepare information?						
Did he have sales aids prepared and checked?						
2 *Opening interview* Did he gain attention?						
Did he explore needs?						
Did he get customer talking about his needs?						
3 *Sales presentation* Did he use visual aids?						
Did he match benefits to customer needs?						
Did he anticipate objections?						
Did he get customer involved?						
Did he use simple language?						
4 *Handling objections* Did he recognise objections?						
Did he handle them satisfactorily?						
Did customer accept the answers?						
5 *Close* Did he ask test questions?						
Did he recognise buying signals?						
Did he ask customer for order?						
Did customer order?						
6 *Product knowledge* Did he display a knowledge of the product demonstrated?						

Example 5.1 Appraisal form: BOC OHMEDA

Selling activity	Yes No	Yes No	Yes No	Yes No	Yes No	Comments
Did he use the knowledge effectively?						
Did he display a knowledge of competition to the product?						
Did he use the knowledge effectively?						
7 *Work organisation* Does he write accurate well thought out reports?						
Does he meet deadline with his reports?						
Are his customer records up to date and relevant?						
Does he care for Company car — keep it clean and roadworthy?						
Demonstration equipment Is it used and in good condition?						
Literature — is it used properly and in good presentable condition?						

Representative's comment

Action to be taken as agreed
between representative and RSM

RSM recommendations
(Training needs etc)

Signature . . . .   Signature . . . .
                    RSM   Representative

Example 5.1 Appraisal form: BOC OHMEDA —*concluded*

GEORGE-GOOD
CORPORATION
16720 EAST GALE AVENUE · CITY OF INDUSTRY, CA 91749

APPRAISAL OF SALES PERSONNEL

NAME		TERRITORY No	GEOGRAPHICAL LOCATION THIS APPRAISAL

DATE OF LAST APPRAISAL	DATES WORKED WITH THIS EVALUATION

SUPERVISOR'S OBJECTIVE THIS APPRAISAL

WHAT WAS OBJECTIVE OF LAST APPRAISAL	RESULTS

I PERSONAL HISTORY (OPTIONAL)

AGE	HEIGHT	WEIGHT	MALE ☐ FEMALE ☐	OWN HOME ☐ RENT ☐ BOARD ☐	SENIORITY DATE

☐ SINGLE ☐ MARRIED ☐ DIVORCED ☐ SEPARATED ☐ WIDOWED	NO. OF DEPENDANTS (INCLUDING SELF)	NO. OF CHILDREN	AGES OF CHILDREN	WIFE EMPLOYED ☐ YES ☐ NO

LIST ANY PHYSICAL DEFECTS OR HEALTH PROBLEMS	DO YOU RECOMMEND A PHYSICAL EXAMINATION FOR THIS EMPLOYEE? ☐ YES ☐ NO

LIST ANY ADDITIONAL EDUCATIONAL COURSES TAKEN, DEGREES OBTAINED, SINCE DISCUSSION OF LAST APPRAISAL

II CURRENT RATING

	A OUTSTANDING	B MEETING EXPECTATIONS	C NOT MEETING EXPECTATIONS	D UNSATIS-FACTORY
1. KNOWLEDGE OF COMPANY PRODUCTS, PRICES, AND PROGRAMS				
2. FAMILIARITY WITH INDUSTRY CONDITIONS, IN HIS TERRITORY, KNOWLEDGE OF COMPETITIVE ACTIVITIES, PRICES, ETC.				
3. SALES TECHNIQUE: GENERAL PRESENTATION, ABILITY TO CLOSE ORDERS, AND SALES ABILITY				
4. ARE OBJECTIVES SET FOR EACH CALL?				
5. HANDLING OBJECTIONS				
6. KEEPING INITIATIVE				
7. RELATIONSHIP WITH CUSTOMERS				
8. DOES HE PLAN AND ORGANIZE WORK AND USE TIME WISELY (COVERAGE OF TERRITORY)?				
9. ARE CALL REPORTS PROPERLY FILLED OUT AND MAILED ON TIME?				
10. ARE CUSTOMER'S RECORD SHEETS AND FOLDERS PROPERLY MAINTAINED?				
11. IS HE EFFICIENT ON DETAIL WORK AND FOLLOW-UP?				
12. MAINTAINS AND USES ALL AVAILABLE SAMPLES				
13. NEATNESS OF EQUIPMENT (PRESENTATION BINDER, ORDER FORMS, ETC.)				
14. PERSONAL APPEARANCE (BUSINESS DRESS, NEAT, ETC.)				
15. PERSONALITY AND SELF CONFIDENCE				
16. IS HE A SELF-STARTER?				
17. DOES HE TURN IN AND GET THE MOST OUT OF A FULL DAY'S WORK?				
18. IS HE ENTHUSIASTIC ABOUT HIS JOB?				
19. DOES HE WORK WITH A MINIMUM OF SUPERVISION?				
20. ATTITUDE TO TAKE CONSTRUCTIVE CRITICISM AND USE SAME				
☐ CURRENT OVERALL RATING – SUMMARIZE YOUR CURRENT OVERALL APPRAISAL OF EMPLOYEE USING ABOVE RATING KEY				

III COMMENTS

1. COMMENTS REGARDING THE INDIVIDUAL'S STRONG POINTS	WEAK POINTS

2. HOW CAN THIS SALESMAN'S PERFORMANCE BE IMPROVED?

SALESMAN'S COMMENTS

SIGNATURE OF EMPLOYEE	SIGNATURE OF DISTRICT MANAGER	DATE / /

FORM SD-10(1/80)   WHITE: TO HOME OFFICE
YELLOW: D.M. COPY
PINK: EMPLOYEE COPY

Example 5.2 Appraisal form: George-Good Corporation

Appraisal of Sales Personnel

The George-Good Appraisal of Sales Personnel form is designed for two basic uses.

1. For the salesman's District Manager to identify any weaknesses in product knowledge, sales ability, etc., and then assist and train the salesmen in those areas.
2. For a salesman to appraise himself by identifying his own weaknesses and then train himself or request assistance in those areas.

> Rating Key: A = Outstanding
> B = Meeting Expectations
> C = Not Meeting Expectations
> D = Unsatisfactory

Each question on the Appraisal Form should be checked off in the block that is the nearest match to the above rating key.

The company standards indicate that any ratings below 'B' require additional training or immediate improvement.

I   Product Knowledge

1. Knowledge of company products, prices, and programs

    A. Always able to use product knowledge effectively.
    B. More often than not able to use product knowledge effectively.
    C. Seldom able to use product knowledge effectively.
    D. Unable to use product knowledge effectively.

2. Familiarity with industry conditions in his territory, knowledge of competitive activities, prices, etc.

    A. Very familiar with competitive activity in territory.
    B. Somewhat familiar with competitive activity in territory.
    C. Not very familiar with competitive activity in territory.
    D. Not alert to competitive activity in territory.

II   Selling Technique

3. Sales technique: General presentation, ability to close orders, and sales ability.

    A. Always makes good presentations and attempts to close on each call.
    B. Almost always makes good presentations and attempts to close on each call.
    C. Sometimes has trouble with presentations and closing.
    D. Often has trouble with presentation and closing.

4. Are objectives set for each call?

    A. Always has planned objectives for each call.
    B. Nearly always has planned objectives for each call.
    C. Sometimes has planned objectives for each call.
    D. Seldom has planned objectives for each call.

5. Handling Objections

    A. Always able to handle all objections and turn them into selling points.
    B. Usually capable of handling most objections and turn them into selling points.
    C. Rarely able to turn an objection into a selling point.
    D. Completely unable to handle any objections.

6. Keeping Initiative

    A. Always in control even when refused a commitment.
    B. Nearly always in control even when refused a commitment.
    C. Sometimes in control when refused an order.
    D. Seldom in control when refused an order.

7. Relationship With Customers

    A. Always gets along well with most customers.
    B. Nearly always gets along well with most customers.
    C. Sometimes has trouble in getting along with some customers.
    D. Often has trouble in getting along with some customers.

Example 5.2 Appraisal form: George-Good Corporation *—continued*

III **Work Organization**

8. Does he plan and organize work and use time wisely (Coverage of Territory)?

   A. Always fills out itinerary properly and mails on time.
   B. Always fills out itinerary but should outline objectives better.
   C. Sometimes fills out itinerary and mails on time.
   D. Often late in filling out itinerary.

9. Are Call Reports properly filled out and mailed on time?

   A. Always accurate and mailed on time.
   B. Nearly always accurate and mailed on time.
   C. Sometimes accurate and mailed on time.
   D. Seldom accurate and mailed on time.

10. Are customers record sheets and folders properly maintained?

   A. Always updates records with relevant information after each call.
   B. Always updates records with most information after each call.
   C. Most of time updates records with information after each call.
   D. Seldom updates records with relevant information after each call.

11. Is he efficient on detail work and follow-up?

   A. Always answers memos, office request forms, etc., promptly.
   B. Nearly always answers memos, office request forms, etc., promptly.
   C. Most of time answers memos, office request forms, etc., promptly.
   D. Seldom answers memos, office request forms, etc., promptly.

12. Maintains and uses all available samples

   A. Always has samples available and in good order.
   B. Nearly always has samples available and in good order.
   C. Sometimes has samples available and in good order.
   D. Seldom has samples available and in good order.

13. Neatness of Equipment (Presentation binder, order forms, samples, etc.)

   A. Always available and in excellent condition.
   B. Nearly always available and in excellent condition.
   C. Sometimes available and in excellent condition.
   D. Seldom available and in excellent condition.

IV **Personal Characteristics**

14. Personal Appearance (Business dress, neat, etc.)

   A. Always properly dressed, and in good taste.
   B. Nearly always properly dressed, and in good taste.
   C. Sometimes shoes, hair, etc., need attention.
   D. Often personal appearance needs attention.

15. Personality and Self-confidence

   A. Always amicable and confident when working with customers.
   B. Nearly always amicable and confident when working with customers.
   C. Sometimes amicable and confident when working with customers.
   D. Seldom amicable and confident when working with customers.

16. Is he a self-starter?

   A. Always accepts company programs and starts immediately to achieve them.
   B. Nearly always accepts company programs and starts immediately to achieve them.
   C. Sometimes has difficulty in accepting and getting started on company programs.
   D. Often has difficulty in accepting and getting started on company programs.

17. Does he turn in and get the most out of a full day's work?

   A. Always starts early and uses time efficiently.
   B. Always starts early but use of time could be more efficient.
   C. Sometimes has trouble in efficiently using time.
   D. Often has trouble in effective use of time.

Example 5.2 Appraisal form: George-Good Corporation —*continued*

18. Is he enthusiastic about his job?
    A. Always enthusiastic and aggressive.
    B. Nearly always enthusiastic and aggressive.
    C. Sometimes enthusiastic and aggressive.
    D. Seldom enthusiastic and aggressive.

19. Does he work with a minimum of supervision?
    A. Always handles problems well and needs very little assistance.
    B. Nearly always handles problems well and needs very little assistance.
    C. Sometimes has trouble and should request assistance when needed.
    D. Seldom alert to problems and they tend to get out of hand.

20. Attitude to take constructive criticism and use same.
    A. Always willing to learn and improve.
    B. Nearly always willing to learn and improve.
    C. Sometimes willing to learn and improve.
    D. Often is not willing to learn and improve.

Example 5.2 Appraisal form: George-Good Corporation —*concluded*

SALESMAN'S FIELD TRAINING PROGRAMME

G-Good   AA-Above Average   BA-Below Average   P-Poor

Date	Company	C/P	Purpose	The Sale Pre-paration				Opening				Fact-finding				Motivation				Sales Present'n				Objection Handling				Closing				Presentation order ✓ ×	R/F A/A F/U
				G	A/A	B/A	P	G	A/A	B/A	P	G	A/A	B/A	P	G	A/A	B/A	P	G	A/A	B/A	P	G	A/A	B/A	P	G	A/A	B/A	P		

Example 5.3 Appraisal form: Kalamazoo Business Systems

47

SALESMAN   GRADE

Product Know-ledge				Comments
G	A A	B A	P	
				Future Action RSM/Salesman
				Future Action RSM/Salesman
				Future Action RSM/Salesman
				Future Action RSM/Salesman
				Future Action RSM/Salesman

Example 5.3 Appraisal form: Kalamazoo Business Systems —*concluded*

CALL EVALUATION AIDE MEMOIRE

DATE . . . .
REPRESENTATIVE . . . .
CUSTOMER . . . .

Selling Activity	Yes	No	Comments
1. **PRE-CALL PLANNING** Was there a specific objective for the call?			
Was the information prepared?			
Was there a call plan?			
Were the sales aids prepared and checked?			
2. **OPENING INTERVIEW** Was the attention gained?			
Were needs explored?			
Was the customer got talking?			
About his needs?			
3. **SALES PRESENTATION** Were visual aids used?			
Was there matching of benefits to customer needs?			
Were objections anticipated?			
Was the customer involved?			
Was simple language used?			
4. **HANDLING OBJECTIONS** Were objections recognised?			
Were objections handled satisfactorily?			
Did customer accept the answers?			
5. **CLOSE** Were test questions asked?			
Were buying signals recognised?			
Was the customer asked for order or other commitment?			
Did customer order or give commitment?			

Example 5.4 Appraisal form: A major oil company

SUMMARY OF TRAINING NEEDS	
NAME:	DATE:
	COMMENTS
1. **PRE-CALL PLANNING** — Overall/Term Objective — Call Objective — Customer Facts — Visual Aids — Other	
2. **SALES INTERVIEW** — Opening — Presentation — Handling Objections — Close — Keeping the initiative — Lead into next call — Other	
3. **POST CALL REVIEW** — Progress towards overall objectives — Was specific objective achieved — Other	

4. **IDENTIFIED TRAINING NEEDS**

5. **AGREED ACTION TO BE TAKEN BY LINE MANAGER AND REPRESENTATIVE**

Example 5.4 Appraisal form: A major oil company —*concluded*

TRAINING EVALUATION

NAME _____

DATE OF JOINING _____

	JAN	FEB	MAR	APR	MAY	JUN	JUL	AUG	SEP	OCT	NOV	DEC
Product Knowledge **IATA Areas**												
Pandair Worldwide 1												
S S T 2												
Import — Carriage 3												
Cartage												
Company Structure												
Personnel												
Competition												
Aerolink												
UK Clearance												
Sales Skills												
Area Planning												
Work Plan												
Opening												
Presentation												
Overcoming objections												
Close												
Follow Up												
Customer Relationship												
Colleague Relationship												
Negotiating — Customers												
— Staff												
Equipment for Day												

Example 5.5 Appraisal form: Pandair

TRAINING EVALUATION

	JAN	FEB	MAR	APR	MAY	JUN	JUL	AUG	SEP	OCT	NOV	DEC
Administration												
Correspondence												
R/O S/L Replies												
Reports — Daily												
— Monthly												
Credit Applications												
Purchase Orders/AWB's												

KEY

1   Exceeds Requirements
2   Meets Requirements
3   Self Improvement Required
4   Training Recommended
5   Time Scheduled for 3 or 4

Example 5.5 Appraisal form: Pandair *—concluded*

REPRESENTATIVE APPRAISAL

Representative . . . .   Date . . . .

KNOWLEDGE		✓	MANAGER'S COMMENTS
1. Major Products	AS		
	SP		
	BS		
	U		
2. Base Products	AS		
	SP		
	BS		
	U		
3. Competitor Products	AS		
	SP		
	BS		
	U		
4. Territory a) Doctors	AS		
	SP		
	BS		
	U		
b) Hospitals	AS		
	SP		
	BS		
	U		
c) Retail Pharmacists	AS		
	SP		
	BS		
	U		
d) Distributors	AS		
	SP		
	BS		
	U		
OPERATIONAL FACTORS			**MANAGER'S COMMENTS**
1. Personal Factors	AS		
	SP		
	BS		
	U		
2. Appearance	AS		
	SP		
	BS		
	U		
3. Punctuality	AS		
	SP		
	BS		
	U		

Example 5.6 Appraisal form: Smith, Kline and French Laboratories Limited (United Kingdom Overseas Group)

OPERATIONAL FACTORS		✓	MANAGER'S COMMENTS
4. Detailing Materials	AS		
	SP		
	BS		
	U		
5. Reporting & Records	AS		
	SP		
	BS		
	U		
6. Equipment	AS		
	SP		
	BS		
	U		
7. Territory Planning a) Doctor Coverage	AS		
	SP		
	BS		
	U		
b) Achievement of Call Targets	AS		
	SP		
	BS		
	U		
SELLING SKILLS			MANAGER'S COMMENTS
1. Use of Interview Time	AS		
	SP		
	BS		
	U		
2. Fluency, Diction, Vocabulary	AS		
	SP		
	BS		
	U		
3. Building Personal Relationship	AS		
	SP		
	BS		
	U		
4. Establishing Business Purpose	AS		
	SP		
	BS		
	U		
5. Exploring Customer Needs	AS		
	SP		
	BS		
	U		

Example 5.6 Appraisal form: Smith, Kline and French Laboratories Limited (United Kingdom Overseas Group)
—continued

SELLING SKILLS		✓	MANAGER'S COMMENTS
6. Determining Acceptable Solutions	AS		
	SP		
	BS		
	U		
7. Committing to Action Plan	AS		
	SP		
	BS		
	U		
8. Handling Objections	AS		
	SP		
	BS		
	U		

General Comments (Summary of main Strengths & Weaknesses)

Action Taken (i.e. how weaknesses are to be improved and how strengths are to be utilised further)

Recommendations (i.e. what specific training should be undertaken)

Manager's Signature

. . . .

Representative's Signature

. . . .

Example 5.6 Appraisal form: Smith, Kline and French Laboratories Limited (United Kingdom Overseas Group)
—continued

UKOG STANDARDS OF PERFORMANCE

KNOWLEDGE

.1. *Major Products/Currently Promoted Products*

AS — Above Standard —
Demonstrates full knowledge of products under current promotion, with good understanding of all product applications and disease areas. Understands and uses current available promotional literature. Knows and uses relevant proof sources competently.

SP — Standard Performance —
Demonstrates adequate product knowledge to cover products under current promotion. Understands major product applications and disease areas. Understands and uses current available promotional literature. Knows and uses some proof sources competently.

BS — Below Standard —
Product knowledge not always adequate for the job. Product applications and disease areas not fully understood. Current promotional literature not fully understood and used correctly. Proof sources not always available or understood.

U — Unsatisfactory —
Obvious lack of knowledge often embarrassing both representative and doctor. Poor understanding of promotional literature. No proof sources available.

2. *Base Products*

AS — Above Standard —
Demonstrates good knowledge of base products and their applications. Knows all strengths of all formulations.

SP — Standard Performance —
Is able to provide generic names, major indications and strengths of the range of base products.

BS — Below Standard —
Can only provide some knowledge of the Company's range of base products.

U — Unsatisfactory —
Lacking in basic knowledge and ignorant of total product range.

3. *Competitor Products*

AS — Above Standard —
Representative demonstrates ability to recognise and discuss *all* competitor products with regard to their strengths and weaknesses. Full knowledge of trade names, generic names, modes of action, dosage and comparative costs relevant to their territory.

SP — Standard Performance —
Representative demonstrates ability to recognise and discuss relevant *major* competitors with regard to their strengths and weaknesses. Knowledge of trade names, generic names of major competitors, action, dosage and comparative costs relevant to the territory. Should have some understanding of minor competitors with regard to their broad classification and comparative cost.

BS — Below Standard —
Representative has difficulty in recognising some of the major competitors and is weak in discussing their relative strengths and weaknesses. Is sometimes exposed by doctor with regard to in-depth knowledge of major competitors. Poor overall knowledge of minor competitors resulting in confusion and misunderstanding.

U — Unsatisfactory —
Representative lacks awareness and knowledge of major competitors relevant to the territory. Little understanding of minor competitors and their classification.

Example 5.6 Appraisal form: Smith, Kline and French Laboratories Limited (United Kingdom Overseas Group)
—continued

4. *Territory*

a) *Doctors*

AS — Above Standard —
Representative is fully aware of the location and accessibility of all General Practitioners and all important Hospital Doctors within the territory. Is fully aware of all new arrivals and departures.

SP — Standard Performance —
Representative is aware of location and accessibility of most General Practitioners and important Hospital Doctors within the territory. Is usually aware of new arrivals and departures.

BS — Below Standard —
Representative shows some lack of knowledge with regard to location and accessibility of General Practitioners and important Hospital Doctors within the territory. Is usually unaware of new arrivals and departures.

U — Unsatisfactory —
Demonstrates poor knowledge of the geography of the territory. Is unaware of the location and accessibility of many of the General Practitioners and Hospital Doctors within the territory.

b) *Hospitals*

AS — Above Standard —
Knows location, geography and accessibility of all hospitals within the territory. Knows how and when to see all senior doctors in the hospital whose specialities coincide with currently promoted products. Has records of current junior doctors, knowledge of clinic times, duty rotas etc. Knows the location of medical secretaries and pharmacy staff and the stocks and usage of SK&F products within the hospital.

SP — Standard Performance —
Knows location, geography and accessibility of important hospitals within the territory. Knows how and when to see most senior doctors in the hospital whose specialities coincide with currently promoted products. Records of junior staff and knowledge of clinic times etc. are sometimes incomplete. Aware of location of pharmacy staff and good knowledge of stocks and usage of SK&F products within the hospital.

BS — Below Standard —
Not familiar with the location, geography and accessibility of some of the hospitals. Lacks full knowledge of accessibility of senior doctors and incomplete records of junior doctors. Poor awareness of pharmacy staff and current stocks and usage of SK&F products within the hospital.

U — Unsatisfactory —
Not familiar with the location, geography and accessibility of major hospitals. Poor knowledge of senior doctors. Ignorant of pharmacy staff and current stocks and usage of SK&F products within the hospital.

c) *Retail Pharmacists*

AS — Above Standard —
Full knowledge of all Retail Pharmacists and their catchment areas. Demonstrates excellent ability to extract information from the pharmacist in terms of current prescribing trends for SK&F products and competitors.

SP — Standard Performance —
Full knowledge of all Retail Pharmacists and their catchment areas. Usually able to obtain information in terms of current prescribing trends for SK&F products and competitors.

BS — Below Standard —
Lack of knowledge with regard to which are the key Retail Pharmacies and the areas covered. Has difficulty in gaining useful information regarding usage and trends.

U — Unsatisfactory —
Poor knowledge of Retail Pharmacies. Cannot obtain useful information from pharmacist.

Example 5.6 Appraisal form: Smith, Kline and French Laboratories Limited (United Kingdom Overseas Group)
—continued

d) *Distributors*

AS — Above Standard —
Maintains regular contact with and has excellent working relationship with distributor staff. Has established good rapport and feedback. Regularly inspects shelves and feeds back information regarding distribution and stocks of SK&F products.

SP — Standard Performance —
Maintains regular contact with and has reasonable working relationship with distributor staff. Has reasonable rapport with owner/manager. Usually inspects shelves but does not always feed back information on distribution and stocks of SK&F products.

BS — Below Standard —
Not enough regular contact. No real rapport with owner/manager. Poor knowledge of distribution and stock movement.

U — Unsatisfactory —
Lack of contact with distributors. No information available regarding stock levels and movement. Not known by distributor staff.

OPERATIONAL FACTORS

1. *Personal Factors*

AS — Above Standard —
Always exhibits cheerfulness, enthusiasm and conviction. Demonstrates real evidence of building good personal relationships with doctors.

SP — Standard Performance —
Usually exhibits cheerfulness, enthusiasm and conviction. Demonstrates evidence of building personal relationships with some doctors.

BS — Below Standard —
Sometimes demonstrates confidence and enthusiasm in front of the doctor but often shows complacency, pessimism or lack of conviction. Has difficulty building relationships with doctors.

U — Unsatisfactory —
A depressing, irritable or arrogant manner which interferes with selling relationship with doctors.

2. *Appearance*

AS — Above Standard —
Appearance always good; well groomed, neat and clean.

SP — Standard Performance —
Appearance usually good; well groomed, neat and clean.

BS — Below Standard —
Occasionally displays an appearance which is not suited to the job ie. too casual, untidy.

U — Unsatisfactory —
Appearance usually unsuitable for the job with regard to clothing, cleanliness or untidiness.

3. *Punctuality*

AS — Above Standard —
Never late for appointments and meetings.

SP — Standard Performance —
Rarely late for appointments and meetings. If late, usually for genuine unavoidable reasons.

BS — Poor planning of appointments and meetings resulting in a tendency to leave things too late. Resulting in lost calls etc. and causing some inconvenience.

U — Unsatisfactory —
Frequently late for appointments and meetings for no valid reason.

Example 5.6 Appraisal form: Smith, Kline and French Laboratories Limited (United Kingdom Overseas Group)
—continued

4. *Detailing Materials*

   AS   — Above Standard —
   Briefcase is always adequately equipped with current detailing material. Up-to-date literature, visual aids, clinical papers and handouts are always readily located in a sufficient quantity for planned interviews and for the occasional chance interview. Sufficient stocks of back-up material carried routinely in car. All materials kept in perfect condition.

   SP   — Standard Performance —
   Briefcase usually adequately equipped with current detailing material. Up-to-date literature, visual aids, clinical papers and handouts are usually readily located in a sufficient quantity for planned interviews but occasionally 'caught-out' by chance interviews. Sufficient stocks of back-up materials usually carried in car. Most materials kept in perfect condition.

   BS   — Below Standard —
   Briefcase not always adequately equipped with current detailing material. Up-to-date literature, visual aids, papers and handouts are insufficient for planned interviews, or items cannot be readily located. Often lacking in stocks carried, resulting in lost opportunities. Literature not always in good condition.

   U   — Unsatisfactory —
   Briefcase often inadequately equipped with current detailing material and poorly packed. Literature often in poor condition.

5. *Reporting and Records*

   AS   — Above Standard —
   Reporting and correspondence always regular and complete. Replies to letters or requests always dealt with promptly. Records always kept accurately, up-to-date and available for inspection.

   SP   — Standard Performance —
   Reporting and correspondence usually regular and complete. Only exceptionally is reporting not punctual or replies to letters and requests incomplete. Records always kept accurately and up-to-date and available for inspection.

   BS   — Below Standard —
   Reporting and correspondence irregular and sometimes incomplete: replies to letters or requests are inadequate. Records sometimes neglected, out-of-date or not available.

   U   — Unsatisfactory —
   Reporting, correspondence and records neglected, inaccurate, out-of-date or not available.

6. *Equipment*

   AS   — Above Standard
   Car regularly serviced and clean. Any faults or damage promptly reported and repaired. All other company equipment maintained in perfect condition.

   SP   — Standard Performance —
   Car usually serviced regularly and generally clean. Any faults or damage reported and repaired. All other company equipment generally maintained in good condition.

   BS   — Below Standard —
   Car seldom cleaned or regularly serviced. Faults and damage not reported or repaired promptly. Other company equipment allowed to deteriorate rapidly.

   U   — Unsatisfactory —
   Car always dirty and in poor mechanical condition, resulting in breakdowns and time off-the-road. Other company equipment mistreated and abused.

7. *Territory Planning*

   a) Doctor Coverage

   AS   — Above Standard —
   Representative has classified all doctors within the territory, and is routinely seeing over 90% 'A' class doctors per cycle.

Example 5.6 Appraisal form: Smith, Kline and French Laboratories Limited (United Kingdom Overseas Group)
—continued

SP — Standard Performance —
Representative has classified all doctors within the territory and is routinely seeing between 80%–90% of 'A' class doctors per cycle.

BS — Below Standard —
Representative has classified majority of doctors within the territory and is routinely seeing between 70%–80% of 'A' class doctors per cycle.

U — Unsatisfactory —
Representative has classified less than 70% of doctors within the territory and is routinely seeing less than 70% of 'A' class doctors per cycle.

b) Achievement of Call Targets

AS — Above Standard —
Representative usually achieves and often exceeds his agreed call targets for all categories of customers within the territory. Shows evidence of a structured daily and weekly call plan.

SP — Standard Performance —
Representative usually achieves agreed call targets for all categories of customers within the territory. Shows evidence of a structured daily and weekly call plan.

BS — Below Standard —
Representative routinely fails to reach agreed target in one or more customer category. No evidence of structured daily and weekly call plan.

U — Unsatisfactory —
Representative consistently fails to reach agreed targets in all customer categories. No evidence of daily and weekly call plan.

SELLING SKILLS

1. *Use of Interview Time*

   AS — Above Standard —
   Maximum use is made of interview time to achieve Company detailing objectives in the first, second and third detail priorities. Representative does not deviate from detail priorities except when forced to by the doctor. Detail priorities are modified for different categories of customers. Always evidence of pre-call planning and post-call analysis.

   SP — Standard Performance —
   Good use is made of interview time to achieve Company detailing objectives in first, second and third detail priorities. Representative occasionally deviates from detail priorities without good reason. Detail priorities are usually modified for different categories of customers. Usually evidence of pre-call planning and post-call analysis.

   BS — Below Standard —
   Time is wasted on occasions. Representative does not seem fully aware of detail priorities and often varies from them for no good reason. Poor evidence of pre-call planning and post-call analysis.

   U — Unsatisfactory —
   Time wasted. Very poor adherance to Company detailing priorities. No evidence of pre-call planning or post-call analysis.

2. *Fluency, Diction, Vocabulary*

   AS — Above Standard —
   Always communicates all information in a clear and concise manner. No evidence of misunderstanding by customers.

   SP — Standard Performance —
   Usually communicates all information in a clear and concise manner. Only occasionally does customer misunderstand.

   BS — Below Standard —
   Communication mostly clear and concise. Sometimes, misunderstandings arise because of poor diction or vocabulary.

Example 5.6 Appraisal form: Smith, Kline and French Laboratories Limited (United Kingdom Overseas Group)
—continued

U   — Unsatisfactory —
Regular problems by the customer in understanding what the representative is saying, due to poor diction or vocabulary, or the inability of the representative to communicate clearly.

3. *Building Personal Relationship*

AS   — Above Standard —
Representative has built good personal relationships with the majority of his customers. He is obviously liked and respected by them. Always recognises cues and uses the skill of 'supporting' to build personal relationships.

SP   — Standard Performance —
Representative has built good personal relationships with some customers, who like and respect him. Usually recognises cues and uses the skill of 'supporting' to build personal relationships.

BS   — Below Standard —
Representative only appears to have built good personal relationships with a few of his customers. Some customers obviously do not like or respect him. Has difficulty recognising cues and using skill of 'supporting'.

U   — Unsatisfactory —
Representative appears to be unwelcome by most of his customers who neither like or respect him. Does not recognise cues and does not understand or use the skill of 'supporting'.

4. *Establishing Business Purpose*

AS   — Above Standard —
Representative always quickly establishes a business purpose without wasting the doctors time. Always recognises cues and uses the skill of 'Stating General Benefits' to establish a business purpose.

SP   — Standard Performance —
Representative usually quickly establishes a business purpose without wasting too much of the doctors time. Usually recognises cues and uses the skill of 'Stating General Benefits' to establish a business purpose.

BS   — Below Standard —
Sometimes wastes doctors and his own time on idle talk before establishing business purpose. Has problems establishing business purpose and is reluctant to do so. Sometimes fails to recognise cues and fails to use the skill of 'Stating General Benefits' to establish a business purpose.

U   — Unsatisfactory —
Often wastes doctors and his own time on idle talk, sometimes never talks business. Has real problems establishing business purpose and is very reluctant to do so. Fails to recognise cues and does not use or understand how to use the skill of 'Stating General Benefits' to establish business purpose.

5. *Exploring Customer Needs*

AS   — Above Standard —
Uses questions intelligently to control the detail towards the objectives set in pre-call planning. Clearly appreciates the difference between open and closed questions and uses each appropriately. Demonstrates variety in opening sequences. Listens carefully to customer's answers to his questions.

SP   — Standard Performance —
Appreciates the difference between open and closed questions and generally uses each appropriately. Questions not always planned to progress the detail towards pre-set call objectives. Occasionally does not listen carefully enough to doctors answers to his questions. Recognises cues and uses skill of 'Probing' intelligently.

BS   — Below Standard —
Poor appreciation of the application of open and closed questions. Uses questions in a haphazard fashion which does not progress the interview towards pre-set objectives. Often fails to listen to the answers to his questions. Often fails to recognise cues for using the skill of 'Probing'.

Example 5.6 Appraisal form: Smith, Kline and French Laboratories Limited (United Kingdom Overseas Group)
—continued

U — Unsatisfactory —
Either fails to use questions at all, or questions used are completely inappropriate. Does not recognise cues and does not understand or use the skill of 'Probing'. Does not appreciate the difference between open and closed questions.

6. *Determining Acceptable Solutions*

AS — Above Standard —
Always determines a solution acceptable to both his own objectives and the doctors needs. Always uses the two steps of firstly 'Proposing a General Solution' and then 'Recommending a Specific Solution'. Always expands his solution with a benefit statement.

SP — Standard Performance —
Usually determines a solution acceptable to both his own objectives and the doctors need. Sometimes fails to use both steps involved in determining acceptable solutions. Sometimes fails to expand his solution with a benefit statement.

BS — Below Standard —
Has difficulty in determining solutions acceptable to both his own objectives and the doctors needs. Fails to use the two steps involved in determining acceptable solutions and does not understand the two step approach. Fails to expand his solution with a benefit statement.

U — Unsatisfactory —
Does not develop acceptable solutions at all. Does not understand the cues and the skills involved in developing acceptable solutions. Does not use benefit statements and does not understand what benefits are.

7. *Committing to Action Plan*

AS — Above Standard —
Always closes the sale by committing the customer to a definite action plan likely to move him closer to using our product. Always tries to overcome delay by projecting the consequences.

SP — Standard Performance —
Always tries to close the sale by committing the customer to an action plan likely to move him closer to using our product. Usually tries to overcome delay by projecting the consequences.

BS — Below Standard —
Has problems closing sales and is reluctant to get commitment from the customer to an action plan. Does not use the two skills of 'Supporting Acceptance' and 'Requesting Commitment'. Accepts delay from the customer and does not attempt to use the skill of 'Projecting' to overcome it.

U — Unsatisfactory —
Has real problems closing sales. Is extremely reluctant to ask for any commitment from the customer. Does not understand the skills used in closing or fails to recognise cues for acceptance. Does not recognise delay or understand the skills to overcome delay.

8. *Handling Objections*

AS — Above Standard —
Always able to overcome satisfactorily all three types of objections i.e. misunderstanding, scepticism and drawback, by using all of the C.S.S. skills involved.

SP — Standard Performance —
Recognises different types of objections and generally manages to overcome them. Understands the C.S.S. skills involved for all three types of objections.

BS — Below Standard —
Has difficulty dealing with objections. Does not always differentiate between types of objection and does not fully understand the C.S.S. skills needed to overcome these objections.

U — Unsatisfactory —
Either completely ignores objections or is completely halted by them. Does not differentiate between types of objections. Does not understand C.S.S. skills involved in overcoming objections.

Example 5.6 Appraisal form: Smith, Kline and French Laboratories Limited (United Kingdom Overseas Group)
—concluded

Van Sales training checklist

Salesman: . . . .   Van No: . . . .   Date: . . . .

Accompanied by: . . . .   Job Title: . . . .

No. of calls made: . . . .

Code: 1 excellent	2 above average				3 below average 4 unacceptable
Appraisal area	1	2	3	4	Action required/remarks
Routine depot work					
Vehicle driving					
Van security					
Van loading					
'Planned call' skill					
Objective setting					
Selling skills:					
— opening					
— presentation					
— selling benefits					
— dealing with objections					
— closing					
— use of records					
Range extension					
Goodwill — customer relations					
Prices and retailer's margins					
Stock control and rotation					
Ordering skill					
Use of sales aids					
Use of merchandising aids					
Merchandising skill					
Administration					
Reporting and trade information					
Salesman's appearance					
Van appearance					
Safety					
Hygiene					
Self appraisal of performance					

Date of next accompaniment: . . . .   Signed: . . . .

Salesman's Signature: . . . .

Example 5.7 Appraisal form: Food, Drink and Tobacco Industry Training Board

Appraisal Guidance Notes

Appraisal area	1 excellent	2 above average	3 below average	4 unacceptable	
Objective setting	Uses record card before call Checks stock in the call Amends objectives based on stocks where necessary Looks for gaps in the range Watches competitors' stocks	Uses record card as a basis for order Sets objectives and tries to achieve them Does not check objectives with stocks	Takes record card into call Not used Tries to sell but sets objectives as he goes along	No objectives Rushes in without any thought Never checks records Sets impossible objectives	
Salesman's appearance	Smart — hands clean Clean — nails clean Neat — hair combed and clean	Quite smart Clean Tends to be untidy	Not very clean Hair, or hands, or nails dirty Untidy	Inappropriately dressed Hands and nails dirty Unkempt hair	
Safety	Parks van in safe position Uses steps at rear Carries weights, using correct lifting techniques Uses sack trucks for heavy loads Is careful on steps	Carries out safety procedures consistently Generally parks vehicle in safe position	Not always careful enough when parking Knows correct procedures but cuts corners Always in a hurry	Parks van in dangerous positions Lifts loads dangerously Jumps from vehicle tailboard carrying goods, etc.	

Example 5.7 Food, Drink and Tobacco Industry Training Board — *concluded*

WAVERLEY VINTNERS LIMITED

FIELD ACCOMPANIMENT STANDARDS (COMPANY STANDARD — B)

PRECALL:

JOURNEY PLAN	—	Has a journey plan for coverage of all calls set out in a logical and economic fashion. Days calls planned to make maximum use of selling time available. Journey Plan adhered to whenever possible.
CALL OBJECTIVE & PLAN	—	Has a plan for each account and an objective for that call which is based on information from record card and current Marketing information. The objective being realistic and attainable.
CALL INFORMATION	—	Always has relevant account and customer information available, i.e. Record Card, Sales Statistics, Sales Aids, Samples and Point of Sale when required in line with call objective.
COMPANY	—	Knows the facts about main Company lines and is able to draw customer benefits from them.
COMPETITOR	—	Knows main competitive brands and their relevant sales strengths.
PREPARATION FOR NEGOTIATION	—	Identifies likely areas for negotiation and sets clear limits on movement possible.

IN-CALL OBSERVATION:

POINT OF SALES	—	Ensures that Own Brand Products are on optics and in best selling positions. Notes Own Brands not on optic or in poor selling positions for future action.
PROMOTIONAL FEATURE	—	Always attempts to get promoted products advertising support at point of purchase.
PRICING	—	Always check Company and competitor's pricing to ensure Company Policy is being implemented and attempts to rectify any deviations from policy.
POINT OF SALE MATERIAL	—	Uses point of sale material to further the sale of Company products and to reinforce Company presence in call.

SALESMANSHIP:

QUESTIONING TECHNIQUE	—	Uses questions, when appropriate, to discover buyer's needs and inhibitions.
PERSONALISED	—	Tailor's presentation to individual customer by selecting the right product, the relevant facts and appropriate Sales Aids.
LOGICAL SEQUENCE	—	Gains attention and interest of buyer and relates benefits to buyer's needs in an easily followed sequence.
SALES AIDS	—	Uses sales aids to reinforce sales points, maintain buyers interest and substantiate claims whenever possible.
HANDLING OBJECTIONS	—	Is able to anticipate, handle and overcome most objections raised by buyers.
BARGAINING ARENA	—	Recognises entry into this area and is able to assess stance taken by customer and respond with his own stated position.
CONCESSION TRADING	—	Able to relate costs and values of concessions made and given to best advantage.
CONTROL OF INTERVIEW	—	Keeps a balanced control of interview and allows buyer to question and participate.
CLOSING	—	Always closes positively using an appropriate closing technique. Remains in control even when refused commitment.
AGREE	—	Always summarises what has been agreed to the full understanding of both parties.

Example 5.8 Field Accompaniment Standards: Waverley Vintners Limited

IN CALL ACTIVITY:

IMPROVE COMPANY — Always takes opportunities to improve Company presence by use
PRESENCE   of P.O.S. etc.

POST-CALL

ANALYSIS OF CALL — Constructively analyses call noting reasons for success as well as
                   for failure.

PLAN FOR NEXT CALL — Records information on record cards and uses to set objective for
                      the next call on the account.

COMMITTEE DISCUSSIONS:

STRUCTURE   — Sets Presentation out in a logical sequence with a strong
PRESENTATION   introduction and makes full use of visual aids to maintain group
                   interest and involvement.

BALANCES   — Maintains a balanced discussion, ensuring all members of group
PARTICIPATION   have their say, while retaining control.

HANDLING OBJECTIONS — Plans for most likely objections in preparation and make use of
                       group situation to turn objections round to benefits.

SUMMARISES   — Summarises whenever possible and appropriate, to ensure group
                   understanding, and retention of control.

WITHDRAWING   — Asks for commitment and anticipates when to leave.

CUSTOMER RELATIONS:

KNOWS AND IS KNOWN — Establishes a working relationship with all people who can
BY DECISION MAKERS   influence decisions.

COMPANY AND   — Always safeguards the Company interest ahead of the customers
CUSTOMER LOYALTY   when required to do so.

SERVICE   — Provides a personal service to customers by keeping them informed
                   on local developments or innovations likely to improve their
                   business.

WORK ORGANISATION:

CUSTOMER RECORD — Keeps record cards up to date with information from previous calls,
CARDS   transfers buying information from stats and any other relevant
                   changes on a call by call basis.

REPORTS ACCURATELY — Submits accurate and relevant reports on time.
AND ON TIME

CREDIT CONTROL   — Ensures all customers operate to Company Policy and informs
                   Management of any credit problems.

CARE OF COMPANY CAR — Good roadworthy condition and clean and tidy.
CARE OF COMPANY — Always carries literature and equipment and maintains it in good
EQUIPMENT AND   condition and up to date.
LITERATURE

A Above Company Standard.
B Company Standard
C Capable of Improvement
D Unacceptable

Example 5.8 Field Accompaniment Standards: Waverley Vintners Limited *—continued*

WVL FIELD ACCOMPANIMENT REPORT

Region: ....
Area: ....
Representative: ....
....

Dates of:
Accompaniment: ....
No of Days Acc.: ....
No of Calls Observed: ....

Section	Item	A	B	C	D	COMMENTS
PRE-CALL	Preparation/Planning					
	– Journey Plan					
	– Call Objective & Plan					
	– Call Information					
	– Company					
	– Competitor					
	– Preparation for Negotiation					
In Call Observation	WV Presence					
	– Point of Sale					
	– Promotional Feature					
	– Pricing					
	– Point of Sale Material					
SALESMANSHIP	– Questioning Technique					
	– Personalised					
	– Logical Sequence					
	– Sales Aids					
	– Handling Objections					
	– Bargaining Area					
	– Concession Trading					
	– Control of Interview					
	– Closing					
	– Agree					
	– Improve Company Presence					
Post In-Call Call Activity	– Analysis of Call					
	– Plan for Next Call					
Committee Discussions	– Structure Presentation					
	– Balances Participation					
	– Handling Objections					
	– Summarises					
	– Withdrawing					
Customer Relations	– Knows and is Known by Decision Makers					
	– Company and Customer Loyalty					
	– Service					
Work Organisation	– Customer Record Cards					
	– Reports Accurately and on time					
	– Credit Control					
	– Care of Company Car					
	– Care of Company Equipment & Literature					

STRENGTHS:

IMPROVEMENT AREAS:

TRAINING CARRIED OUT (Content & Technique):

FUTURE ACTION:

COMMENTS ON PERFORMANCE SINCE LAST ACCOMPANIMENT:

Signed:
....
Representative

Signed:
....
Assessor

9051 0285

Example 5.8 Field Accompaniment Standards: Waverley Vintners Limited—*concluded*

WHEN TO USE AN APPRAISAL SYSTEM

The appraisal system discussed in this chapter is essentially a tool to be used by the field sales manager and the sales personnel who report to him. Other personnel who might use it, with the approval of the manager and the salesmen, would need to be restricted probably to a field sales trainer, a sales colleague or sales training officer

This system is designed to be used under *four* sets of circumstances.

New salesmen

The first use of the system is for new salesmen at the completion of their initial field training (this is dealt with in detail in Chapter 10). The completed form provides the manager and the new salesman with an *initial* assessment of specific strengths and weaknesses and pinpoints where subsequent training and development will need to be concentrated.

Experienced salesmen

The system should also be used to appraise an experienced salesman. (defined in chapter 11 How to train the Experienced Salesman). The field sales manager should complete a form at the end of every field training visit to *every* experienced salesman reporting to him (this is dealt with in Chapter 11). A word of caution for those managers who accompany each of their salesmen as often as once every five or ten working days. Beware of the danger of carrying out a field appraisal so frequently that there is little or no difference between one appraisal and another. This is analogous to the impatient gardener who, having planted a young sapling, digs up the roots every day to see if they are growing. They never will.

All Salesmen – self-appraisal

The third set of circumstances concerns all salesmen. Since I wrote the first edition of *Training Salesmen on the Job* in 1975, a large amount of evidence has been accumulated that indicates that most people are able to assess their own past work performance.[1] Indeed, no matter what appraisal system you use, your salesmen have their own views about how well or badly they have performed and your appraisals will be received against this background anyway.

When an individual's self assessment is harnessed to specific aspects of work performance, there tends to be greater honesty and objectivity. The evidence here shows that an individual's assessments of his performance are more discriminating and less lenient than those of his manager. Consequently appraisals based on such self-assessments are likely to be much more effective. Such assessments concentrate on developing strengths and correcting weaknesses. The greater the involvement of the individual in identifying personal strengths and weaknesses increases his or her willingness to implement the follow up action required. Self-appraisal then by salesmen is the most effective way to ensure that personal follow-up action takes place; 'the orders we most obey are those we give ourselves'.

Taking all these factors together, it is an important part of the field sales manager's job to both encourage self-appraisal and to train his sales personnel in how to appraise themselves. Each salesman should complete a self-appraisal at regular agreed intervals between field training visits and send a copy to his manager to indicate his assessment of his current performance. Further guidance is given on this in the chapters on how to train *new* and *experienced* salesmen.

1. Meyer, H. H. 'Self-Appraisal of job performance', *Personnel Psychology*, 33, 1980.
    Thornton, G. C. 'Psychometric properties of self appraisals of job performance', *Personnel Psychology*, 33, 1980.

All salesmen – annual appraisal

The annual appraisal of each salesman can be linked to the on-the-job appraisal system described in this chapter. When reviewing six or twelve months' performance, there is always the danger of the manager being influenced favourably or otherwise by what psychologists call 'the recency of events'. For example, one salesman may have had an unsatisfactory year's performance, then a 'windfall' order that he had little or nothing to do with obtaining, comes in in the last month of the year. As a result he overachieved his sales target. Another salesman has an outstanding year's work but is off the road for the last five weeks of the financial year because he crashed his company car.

When a field sales manager is preparing for the biannual or annual performance appraisal of his salesmen, the *individual* field appraisal forms completed *throughout* the year provide an inventory of progress or otherwise and a factual aide-memoire to assist discussion and objectivity and support the giving or withholding of any merit rises. They also act as a check against the manager being too biased by a recent event either favourable or unfavourable to the salesman.

HOW TO RATE SALES PERFORMANCE

One of the major weaknesses of most appraisal systems is the *absence* of rating scales linked to precisely worded, laid down standards which have been agreed and accepted by all who will be applying them. The purpose of such rating scales is a simple one. To establish the *facts* about performance and to minimise emotional feelings and opinion. Any words to be used as labels to define given standards of performance must be chosen with great care. If, for example, your appraisal system uses words such as *very good; above average* or *weak* without defining them, they will mean different things to different people. Many managers have said that they do not like the word *satisfactory* as a top rating in a sales performance appraisal. They would rather use *excellent*. Putting aside personal views in favour of one or the other, let us look at the dictionary definitions:

Satisfactory: adequate, meeting all needs, desires, or expectations.
Excellent: Surpassing others in some good quality.

The two words are very different in their meanings. So it is essential to define appraisal standards as precisely as possible so that there is little or no room for differences of opinion or of interpretation.

The rating scales to be used in the salesman performance appraisal have been constructed so that what the salesman actually does is linked precisely to the ratings made against each performance factor. These rating guidelines are shown in Figure 5.4. Now let us apply these rating scales to actual field accompaniment. Using the form shown in Figure 5.2 the sales manager, observing a salesman making ten selling calls has decided to concentrate on two performance factors, the salesman's call preparation and his care of the company's sales literature which he should use as an important visual support when selling. Dependent upon the facts revealed before and during each of these ten selling calls, the manager would then rate them as satisfactory, above average, below average or unsatisfactory as shown in Figure 5.5. The end result is a qualitative and quantitative rating in two areas of work performance that the manager and salesman can use to pinpoint a training need.

Factor appraised	Rating	Rating basis
Product knowledge		
Company/competitor	S	Always able to use product knowledge effectively
	AA	More often than not able to use product knowledge effectively
	BA	Seldom able to use product knowledge effectively
	U	Completely unable to use product knowledge effectively
Selling technique		
Preparation	S	Always plans each call using information from previous calls on his record card
	AA	More often than not plans each call using information from previous calls on his record card
	BA	Seldom plans each call using information from previous calls on his record card
	U	Never plans each call using information from previous calls on his record card
Opening	S	Always uses a planned opening for every call
	AA	Nearly always uses a planned opening for every call
	BA	Seldom uses a planned opening for any call
	U	Never uses a planned opening for any call
Sales presentation	S	Always mentions need based benefits on every call
	AA	More often than not mentions need based benefits on every call
	BA	Seldom mentions need based benefits on any call
	U	Never mentions any benefits on any call
Objection handling	S	Always able to handle all objections and turn them into selling points
	AA	Usually capable of turning most objections around to produce benefits
	BA	Rarely able to turn an objection into a selling point
	U	Completely unable to handle any objections
Closing	S	Always closes on every pre-set objective
	AA	More often than not closes on every pre-set objective
	BA	Seldom closes on any pre-set objective
	U	Never closes at all

Figure 5.4 Salesman performace rating scales

Factor appraised	Rating	Rating basis
Keeping initiative	S	Always in control even when refused a commitment
	AA	Nearly always in control when refused a commitment
	BA	Seldom in control when refused an order
	U	Never in control when refused an order
Work organisation		
Accurate reports	S	Always accurate
	AA	Nearly always accurate
	BA	Seldom accurate
	U	Never accurate
Regular reports	S	Always meets deadlines
	AA	Nearly always meets deadlines
	BA	Seldom meets deadlines
	U	Never meets deadlines
Customer record cards	S	Always up-dates records with relevant information from previous call
	AA	Nearly always up-dates records with relevant information from each call
	BA	Seldom up-dates records with relevant information from previous call
	U	Never up-dates record cards from previous calls
Care of the company car	S	Always excellent roadworthy condition, always clean and tidy
	AA	Good roadworthy condition, usually clean and tidy
	BA	Roadworthy but seldom in clean and tidy condition
	U	Poor roadworthy condition; never clean and tidy
Care of equipment	S	Always available and in excellent condition
	AA	Nearly always available. Usually in good condition
	BA	Seldom available. Condition often poor
	U	Never has relevant equipment. Condition unsatisfactory
Care of literature	S	Always has literature and in excellent condition
	AA	Nearly always has literature and usually in good condition
	BA	Seldom has literature and condition often poor
	U	Never has literature maintained in satisfactory condition

Rating scale: S = Satisfactory, AA = Above average, BA = Below average, U = Unsatisfactory

Figure 5.4 Salesman performance rating scales — *concluded*

Evaluate	S	A A	B A	U	Rating Basis
1. PRODUCT KNOWLEDGE					
2. SELLING TECHNIQUE					
Call preparation	✓				Always plans each call using relevant data
		✓			More often than not 8/10 plans each call, etc.
			✓		Seldom plans each call 3/10, etc.
				✓	Never plans any call 0/10, etc.
3. SALES ADMINISTRATION	✓				Always has literature and in excellent condition
Care of literature		✓			Nearly always has literature 7/10
			✓		Seldom has literature 2/10, condition often dirty
				✓	Never has relevant literature

Figure 5.5 Evaluating salesman performance on the job

COMMON ERRORS IN APPRAISING PEOPLE

There are many pitfalls in completing performance appraisals. Any appraisal system is only as good as the competence and objectivity of those doing the appraisal. It is difficult to discount the influence our fellow men have upon us. The most common errors to bear in mind are:

1 A willingness to appraise salespeople who may be virtually unknown to the appraiser.
2 An unwillingness to take the time or make the effort needed to analyse individual performance thoroughly. This means that field training itself cannot be a whistle-stop affair lasting an hour or so.
3 The danger of being either over-friendly or over-critical. It is very easy to slip into the field of opinion, surmise and prejudice. Make sure that facts always back up ratings wherever possible.
4 The tendency to regard those we like as excellent in every department of their performance; those we dislike as being deficient in every department of their performance.
5 Reluctance to make adverse appraisals because we fear they must be discussed with the salesperson appraised.
6 The lack of uniform standards of performance. Words do not always mean the same thing to the field sales manager and to the salesperson.
7 Reluctance to rate salesmen high or low and the desire to stick to the safety of 'good' or 'average'. It is well known that if people are asked to rate candidates out of five categories, most will use the middle category. This tendency often slips into appraisals – hence the exclusion of the rating 'average'; this word is no help in trying to make a decision.

CONCLUSION

The regular appraisal on the job is the only means by which the salesman and his field sales manager can measure and agree performance standards relating to 'what is done during the call'. The success of any appraisal system really depends on three things.

First, it is important that there are *no secrets* about the appraisal. Appraisals are completed with the salesman, the contents, actions and changes are agreed and recorded by the salesman and manager.

Second, establish and use *agreed rating scales* which help the salesman and manager to pinpoint an area of knowledge or skill that is affecting performance and needs attention.

Third, encourage each of your salesmen to *appraise themselves* on a regular basis. How this appraisal system is used to develop the knowledge, selling skills and effective performance of new and experienced salesmen is examined in greater detail in the chapters relating to those two on-the-job training activities.

Action planning checklist

	Answers	Action and timing
1 Does the company have a salesman performance appraisal system (see Figure 5.3)? If not, when is a system going to be designed and by whom?		
2 Has the field sales management been trained in how to appraise salesmen performance on the job? If not, what steps will be taken to ensure managers are trained?		
3 Are the salespeople told about the company salesman performance appraisal system when they join the company? If not, what point does the system serve to improve performance?		
4 If the salespeople are aware of the company's appraisal system do they use it as well as the field sales manager to appraise their own sales performance?		

6:

How to Identify Sales Training Needs

The starting point for planning and carrying out effective training of the salesmen on an individual basis is the careful and precise identification of training needs. So much well-intentioned but general sales training has fallen upon stony ground because to the salesmen at the receiving end it did not appear to be tailored to their needs or to take account of the special selling situations they faced. In one company employing a large sales force the general sales manager decreed that all field sales managers would follow a set sequence in training salesmen on the job each month. Thus in month one every salesman was trained in how to prepare a call, in month two how to open the sales interview, and so on. This satisfied this general sales manager's need because he wanted the security and simplicity of such a control. But as an approach to training it failed because it took no account of individual training needs.

SIX LOGICAL STEPS IN TRAINING-NEEDS ANALYSIS

The training needs of salesmen should be analysed in six steps:

1 Defining the job to be done, the specific tasks involved and the performance standards required. This involves writing a job description. Examples of job descriptions are illustrated in Figures 6.1, 6.3 and 6.5.

2 Specifying what knowledge, skills and attitudes are needed to achieve the standards set for the job. The definition of what knowledge is needed is relatively easy. It is much more difficult to specify the skills needed and the level of performance of those skills. For example, to say that a salesman should be able 'to organise his sales calls effectively' is not as helpful or as measurable as 'to plan to make the most profitable use of time so as to maintain a daily average call rate of eight calls of which two will be prospect calls'. Based upon the draft job description for an agricultural representative, a training needs analysis setting out the knowledge, skills and attitudes required as shown in Figure 6:2 should be completed. Figure 6.4 shows a completed analysis for the medical representative.

The representative will be required to:

1 Work with his manager and through MBO to establish effective sales plans and to maximise his contribution to them

2 Carry out the agreed plans by working integrally with key merchant distributors in his area and by establishing detailed working plans with them

3 Make effective personal sales contact with the most worthwhile potential customers on a continuous and up-dated basis

4 Provide the after-sales service which is necessary to maintain existing business and to do this as far as possible through planned delegation to the distributors

5 Personally investigate all quality complaints and follow them through to a satisfactory settlement

6 Identify, agree and fulfill the motivation and training needs of distributors' representatives which are necessary to enable them to increase and service their sales

7 Ensure that all information on competitors' activities is passed promptly and accurately to his manager

8 Working with and through distributors, support all company promotional activities relevant to his area and participate effectively in meetings and demonstrations as requested

9 Maintain and establish contacts with ancillary companies and organisations and liaise with them to mutual advantage

10 Continuously identify and up-date the commercial and technical knowledge necessary to carry out all aspects of the job to the highest standard

Figure 6.1 A draft job description (Agricultural Representative)

3 Defining what knowledge, skills and attitude each salesman has, how and what performance standards each is achieving. The collection of this information requires the setting up and constant use of an effective salesman performance appraisal system. How this is instituted is the subject of Chapter 7. It also involves agreement on measurement standards and techniques. An example of standards related to key tasks for a salesman is illustrated in Figure 8:2.

4 Defining the training gap in each knowledge, skill, attitude area.

5 Defining what additional training needs arise as a result of changes external to the salesman's past achievements and standards. This necessitates checking on a systematic and continuous basis the directions and future plans for the company's marketing planning and sales promotion and its sales planning and recruitment functions; for example, a decision to increase or reduce the overall size of the sales force could involve every salesman in revising his methods of working and call frequencies, thus giving rise to a new training need in the field. It is necessary to relate the company's future plans to its current sales force needs and to ensure that all such changes and the training needs they give rise to are identified and co-ordinated on a continuous basis.

6 Defining the training priorities for the current period. There is always more to do than there is the time or the people to do it. So the field sales manager has to identify what are the training needs in the immediate future, in the mid-term and in the long-term. Peter Drucker, in *The Effective Executive* in a chapter titled 'First things First', said: 'The reason why so few executives concentrate is the difficulty of setting ''posteriorities'' – that is deciding what tasks not to tackle – and sticking to the decision.'

Job description item	Task	Knowledge	Skills	Attitudes
Make effective sales contact	(a) Plan journeys	Geography Market days/events Whether appointments are needed	Ability to assess timing of individual calls Ability to plan journeys economically	Time and effort saved makes work easier, enjoyable and effective
	(b) Plan calls	Customer needs Products available Distributor involvement Customer attitude	Ability to identify customer needs Communication with distributors	
	(c) Make effective sales presentations	Product and system knowledge Economics Customer needs Selling techniques/negotiation Sales benefits Nature of objections Alternative methods of closing	How to open an interview How to create interest How to present benefits How to overcome objections How to close positively Negotiation	Professional selling is essential in our competitive market
	(d) Involve management when necessary	Own limitations of authority Customer needs Price limitations	Communication with management and distributors	A team works better than a collection of individuals
Keep technically and commercially up-to-date	(a) Read farming press and technical journals	What knowledge and skills are needed as defined by: the job, the company, the district, and change	Ability to: self-train, learn and apply, interpret information, and use initiative	Training is not a classroom operation
	(b) Attend relevant meetings and events			Good training is self-inspired, continuous and accumulative
	(c) Assess own training needs with manager on a continuous basis			
Liaise with ancillary companies and organisations	(a) Make contact with their representatives	Who they are Where they operate Who they know Who knows them Mutual contacts	Establish mutual respect Sell self Establish mutual benefits	We need all the extra 'salespeople' we can get
	(b) Maintain contact to mutual advantage	As above	Work together to mutual benefit	

Figure 6.2 Agricultural representative's job description — task/knowledge/skills/attitudes analysis

Job description item	Task	Knowledge	Skills	Attitudes
Support promotional activities and participate in meetings/ demonstrations	(a) Apply promotional plans in own district	Company plans Area plans District plans Distributor needs Farmer needs	Selling of promotion to: distributors, distributor representatives, and farmers	Distributors distribute Representatives sell Farmers use
	(b) Take part in meetings and demonstrations	Suitable venues Suitable speakers Meeting organisation Press coverage Chairmanship Products/systems Company policy	Public speaking Discussion leading Chairmanship Organisation Report writing	We are professionals
Internal communication	(a) Report competitor activities to management	Competitors' representatives Competitors' customers Competitors' products Policies	Accurate report writing Objective interpretation Communication with third parties	Effective action depends on accurate and balanced reportage
Sales planning	(a) Identify target: farmers	Number of units Sizes Location Present situation/usage Future needs Finance	Ability to select priorities Good administration	Time, effort and thought given to planning make the whole job easier, more enjoyable, and more effective
	(b) Draw up action plans	Company activities Competitor activities Distributor involvement Timing Farm situations Management assistance available Own time available	Good communication with managers and distributors Ability to set realistic objectives in a reasonable time scale	An agreed plan of action makes success more likely

Figure 6.2 Agricultural representative's job description — task/knowledge/skills/attitudes analysis — *continued*

Job description item	Task	Knowledge	Skills	Attitudes
	(c) Plan with distributors	Distributor coverage / Distributors' representatives / Credit problems / Distributor needs	Motivation of distributor representatives	Liaison is essential for success
Motivate and train distributors	(a) Identify needs for each distributor and each representative	Company needs / Individual needs / Farmer needs } Priority 'gaps' to be filled	Distinguish between knowledge, skills and attitudes and establish priorities / Distinguish between 'lack of' and 'need for'	Efficient profitable distribution is essential to our own prosperity
	(b) Agree what should be done and by whom	Methods of training / Other facilities available / Other personnel available / Own limitations / Own skills	Liaise with management / 'Sell' training to distributor and representatives / Planning and preparation / Setting of objectives	It is our responsibility to equip our distributors with the knowledge and skill to sell products and services
	(c) Carry out training	Methods: on-the-job, off-the-job / Product knowledge / Sales knowledge / Use of training techniques / Preparation of aids / Appropriate location	Applying the right method / Translating knowledge to suit audience / Using training techniques / Using training aids	Training is not only a classroom operation. Use of the right method and careful preparation essential
	(d) Evaluate on a continuous basis	Objectives set / Objectives achieved } Gap	Interpret reason for gap / Take appropriate steps, ie change objectives, change training method and change training content, as necessary	All good training is continuous and accumulative
Provide after-sales service	(a) Identify what is needed (i) For personal action (ii) For distributor action	Priorities / Customer needs / Customer attitude / Distributor coverage	Ability to select priorities / Ability to designate	

Figure 6.2 Agricultural representative's job description — task/knowledge/skills/attitudes analysis — *continued*

Job description item	Task	Knowledge	Skills	Attitudes
	(iii) For individual customers	Representative's ability		
	(b) Keep personal involvement to a minimum	As above	Tactful delegation to distributor representatives Training of representatives	
	(c) Provide first-class personal service where necessary	Technical knowledge Product knowledge Housing Feeding Nutrition Management Finance Economics	Ability to present service effectively Use as a sales aid	Service is a tool to be used in gaining and maintaining trade, not an end in itself
Investigate quality complaints	(a) Investigate the situation on the farm	Character of customer Distributor involved Representative involved Methods of: feeding, management, housing, feed storage and delivery Disease factors Product knowledge	Look at problem objectively Assess likely cause Assess any loss tactfully and accurately Establish genuine rapport with the customer	A quality complaint is an opportunity to build customer confidence and loyalty
	(b) Report back to management	As above, plus: Tonnage involved Mill origin Date of delivery and manufacture Interpretation of situation Recommendation for action	Accurate report writing Accurate interpretation of facts, people and circumstances Empathetic presentation of information	The customer should neither lose nor gain if the complaint is handled correctly
	(c) Conclude complaint satisfactorily	Laboratory report Interpretation of report Character of customer Relation between loss and views of company and customer Closing an interview	Selling skills in presenting information Obtaining agreement without haggling Positive closing	The customer should feel that his complaint has been handled fairly, speedily, and sympathetically

Figure 6.2 Agricultural representative's job description — task/knowledge/skills/attitudes analysis — *concluded*

79

Job Title: MEDICAL REPRESENTATIVE — GENERAL

Department: Pharmaceutical Marketing

Job Objective: To increase the market share of the Company's products in the therapeutic groups in which the Company is competing. Specific product objectives are stated at regular intervals in the selling schedule.

Responsible to: AREA MANAGER

Duties:

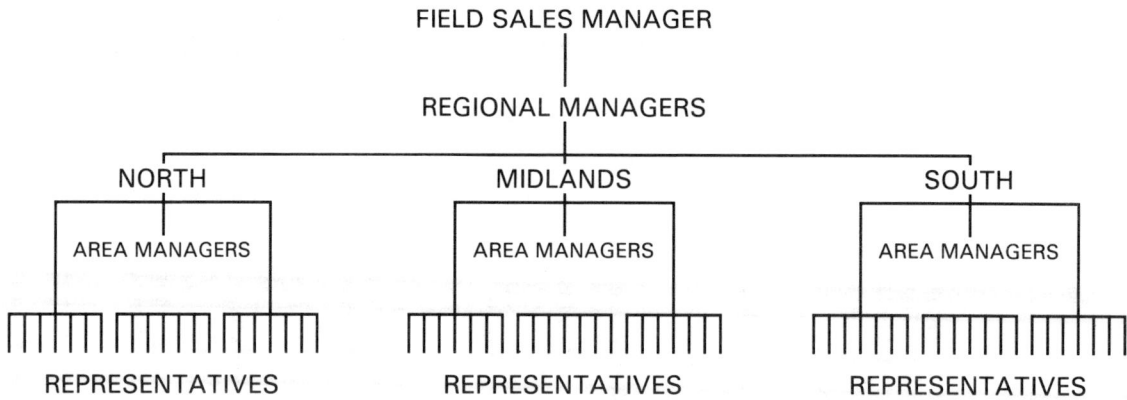

FIELD SALES MANAGER

REGIONAL MANAGERS

NORTH	MIDLANDS	SOUTH
AREA MANAGERS	AREA MANAGERS	AREA MANAGERS
REPRESENTATIVES	REPRESENTATIVES	REPRESENTATIVES

PRESCRIBED

1 To organise the working of the territory to ensure that all potentially good prescribers are visited at regular intervals with the most economical use of time and mileage.

2 To plan each cycle, week, day and visit to make the most effective use of interview time.

3 To make the most effective presentation of the Company's products at each type of call in order to persuade doctors and others who influence the choice of medication to recommend specific products.

4 To maintain an up-to-date record card file of doctors (by constant reference to Executive Council lists, etc.) and ancillary staff, with information on the best time and method of interviewing customers, and all relevant information on the customer, together with pertinent reports on each call.

5 To maintain standards of general medical and product knowledge by studying communications from the office, medical journals and reprints, and training material provided.

6 To obtain and communicate to the office through Field Management information regarding customers, and competitors' activities.

7 To attend Regional and Area Meetings, Sales Conferences, Medical Exhibitions, Training and Refresher courses, as requested.

8 To maintain the Company equipment — car, briefcase, literature, samples, etc. — in good order.

9 To co-operate with the Medical and Market Research Departments and carry out trials and surveys as and when requested.

10 To report in detail at prescribed intervals on progress and developments in the territory and to put forward suggestions which may help to increase sales or efficiency of the Company.

11 To promote the Company's interests in all ways, including arranging for Company films to be shown to medical audiences, attending meetings whenever possible and speaking at meetings if requested.

Figure 6.3 Medical representative's job description

12 To maintain an acceptable standard of appearance.

13 To maintain the prestige and reputation of the Company by setting high personal standards of behaviour and integrity.

14 To visit Retail and Hospital Pharmacists and Wholesalers to endeavour to ensure that adequate and up-to-date stocks of Company products are maintained, and to deal with enquiries and complaints.

DISCRETIONARY

To follow up speculative leads in product information and usage that may emerge and be relevant to the job objective, keeping his superior and any appropriate departments informed.

Limits of Authority:

1 No authority to alter prices, discounts, negotiate contracts or delivery dates without prior reference to Sales Department.

2 Not to undertake to provide stocks for clinical trials without prior approval of the Area Manager.

3 May supply limited stocks of products for personal assessment by doctors.

4 May purchase office supplies and stationery for use in occupation up to a limit of £10 without prior approval of Manager.

5 Car travel to be in accordance with the Company's operating scale.

6 Authorised travel at second class rate.

7 Overnight accommodation to be up to the standard of 3-star hotel.
Dinner at the rate of hotel table d'hôte menu. Lunch expenditure up to £2.50 per day.

8 After the first year with the Company, may entertain special customers to lunch or dinner.

9 May provide entertainment, refreshments, etc., at meetings and film shows with prior approval of Area and Regional Managers.

10 May claim half telephone rental, and all business calls.

Figure 6.3 Medical representative's job description —*concluded*

Ability	Knowledge	Level	Skill	Level	Attitude
To organise work	Geographical knowledge of area	E	Planning of week/day/call	E	Positive attitude that planning creates selling opportunities
	Intimate knowledge of surgeries, hospitals, OP's Homes, clinics, pharmacies, wholesalers	E	Planning of visits to coincide with GP and hospital calls to ensure supplies of products to meet prescriptions	E	Avoidance of wastage of time and money
	Knowledge of doctors, pharmacists, nursing staff, their hobbies, interests and recent achievements	E	Organisation of information on products and customers	E	Cost consciousness
To record and communicate to Marketing Office	Company's reporting procedure — forms, record cards	E	Finding the right information to record with a minimum of time and effort	E	Belief that communication is important area in making the sales force an effective unit
	Medical Directories, Outpatient Clinic lists	E	Communicating effectively with the Company	E	
	Sales records and SDA	E	Concise and effective written communication	E	
To form a group relationship with members of the Regional team	Sales performance of the Regional team and knowledge of the team	E	Human relationships	E	
			Empathy		
To work unsupervised	Individual sales objectives and individual sales performance	E	Organising and working in an effective manner to meet sales objectives	E	Self-starting, self-motivating
To learn	How to organise information	P	Intellectual skill. Ability to recall and collate information in relevant technical discussions	P	A positive attitude to technical learning

Figure 6.4 Medical representative's job description — task, knowledge/skills/attitudes analysis

Ability	Knowledge	Level	Skill	Level	Attitude
Selling	Basic anatomy, physiology, bacteriology, pathology, pharmacology, and therapeutics	A	Effective presentation of Company's products	E	Belief in contribution of the Company's products to the treatment of disease
	Pharmacology of therapeutic groups of the Company's products	P			
	Diseases which the groups are used to treat	P			
	Pharmacology, chemistry, formulations, indications, contra-indications and side effects, packaging, dosage, and price of Company products	E			
	Scientific papers	E	Reinforcing the presentation with authoritative opinion	E	Belief that papers are an outside objective product assessment
	Techniques of communication	E	Persuasive communication	E	Determination to be professionally competent as a salesman
	Selling techniques	E	Identifying needs	E	Belief that selling is a worthwhile occupation
	Making a structured presentation	E	Opening the sale	E	
	Buying motives	E	Creating a demand	E	Positive approach
	Knowledge of Company history, background and sales objectives as a whole and of promotion methods	E	Satisfying the need	E	Business objectiveness
			Overcoming objections		Integrity, initiative and enthusiasm
			Obtaining commitments		
	Knowledge of the pharmaceutical industry and NHS	F	Empathy	E	Loyalty to and identification with Company
	Knowledge of literature and selling aids	E	Presenting the industry's case in a positive manner	P	Belief that the industry is making contribution to Nation's health and welfare
			Utilising literature and selling aids	E	

Figure 6.4 Medical representative's job description – task, knowledge/skills/attitudes analysis – *concluded*

(A – appreciation, P – practitioner, E – Expert)

Waverley Vintners Ltd

JOB DESCRIPTION

JOB TITLE: .... TERRITORY SALESPERSON ....

AREA: ....

BASE: ....

JOB HOLDER: ....

RESPONSIBLE TO: .... AREA SALES MANAGER ....

LOCATION: ....

SIGNED: .... **DATE:** ....
(Job Holder)

APPROVED BY: .... **DATE:** ....
(Manager)

APPROVED BY: .... **DATE:** ....
(Senior Manager)

1 MAIN JOB OBJECTIVES

Brief description of the major function of the position.

To develop and expand the profitable sale of the Company's products through all available outlets in accordance with set objectives.

KEY RESULT AREAS:
(1)   Territory Volume
(2)   Own/Prop. Product Mix
(3)   Number Existing Customers.
(4)   Number New Customers.
(5)   Territory Objectives.
(6)   Capital Equipment performance.
(7)   Call Rate.
(8)   Evenings Worked.
(9)   Wine Lists.

Figure 6.5 Wine trade salesperson's job description and job specification

2 MAIN RESPONSIBILITIES

List the major tasks of the position, outlining areas where decisions or recommendations are made:

1. To plan and organise his/her activities to ensure effective sales contact throughout their territory.

2. To foster and develop individual personal relationships with Beer Company Representatives in order to identify and exploit mutual opportunities.

3. To recommend and agree a Sales Activity Plan including promotional monies and loan expenditure which will ensure the achievement of the set Territory Objectives.

4. To be aware of Market trends, products and product developments and to understand the implications of these factors for his/her territory.

5. To plan and organise call coverage which will enable Telesales personnel to provide effective and complimentary customer sales contact.

6. To sell and promote WVL and Prop. brands in order to achieve Territory Mix and Distribution Objectives.

7. To ensure all Company Capital Equipment achieves target volume throughput and this, where necessary, is re-sited to realise this.

8. To develop relationship with peers, Sales Management and all related Departments to ensure the communication of mutually relevant information.

9. To maintain a cost-effective control over personal expenses and to report details of entertainment, travelling and other expenditure accurately and regularly as required by Management.

10. To maintain all allocated Company equipment, including Car, in a clean and serviceable condition at all times. To ensure that sales kit and presenters are up-to-date as well as properly maintained.

11. To be available to work such hours as required by the Company.

LIMITS OF AUTHORITY:

1. The Salesperson has authority to accept only those sales which come within the Company's established Pricing, Discount and Credit Control procedures.

2. Authority to request installations of Capital Equipment that fall within the Company's volume criteria for such equipment.

SPECIAL RELATIONSHIPS:

1. Customers at all levels.

2. Special Account customers at Manager's discretion.

3. Contact by personal call, telephone or letter with decision makers or people who directly affect decision making.

4. Telesales, to ensure a common sales strategy for individual customers.

5. Key Account Manager, to report on individual potential and existing major accounts in order to identify potential business and to review performance against standards agreed with the key Account Manager.

Figure 6.5 Wine trade salesperson's job description and job specification —*continued*

PERFORMANCE APPRAISAL:

1. Regular, field-based appraisal of inter-personal skills, selling techniques and plans carried out by the Area Sales Manager.

2. Annual appraisal by ASM covering all aspects of overall achievements against Job Standard Objectives and Development.

3 ORGANISATION AND CONTROL

Draw an organisation chart indicating reporting and organisational relationships:

4 OUTSIDE CONTACTS

Describe contacts made outside the Company as a normal part of the job. Indicate the frequency and the nature of the contacts and the positions of the people contacted. This should be examples, not an exhaustive list.

Figure 6.5 Wine trade salesperson's job description and job specification —*continued*

5 FORMAL QUALIFICATIONS

Indicate the minimum formal education and level of technical or specialist knowledge necessary to achieve satisfactory job performance. This is not necessarily the Job Holder's own qualifications:

Wine & Spirit Higher Certificate.

6 PRACTICAL EXPERIENCE

Indicate the minimum amount of experience considered necessary before satis-factory job performance could be expected:

Figure 6.5 Wine trade salesperson's job description and job specification —*continued*

TERRITORY SALESPERSON – JOB SPECIFICATION

WAVERLEY VINTNERS LIMITED

ITEM	TASK	KNOWLEDGE	SKILL	ATTITUDE
1. TO PLAN AND ORGANISE HIS/HER ACTIVITIES TO ENSURE EFFECTIVE SALES CONTACT THROUGHOUT THE TERRITORY	A. Plan Journeys.	1. Geography. 2. Days Closed. 3. Buyer There? 4. Appointment?	1. Ability to Assess Timing of Calls. 2. Plan Journeys economically.	'A well planned day produces economic use of time and job satisfaction'.
	B. Use of Outlet Information	1. Sales Stats. 2. Record Cards.	1. Ability to interpret trends and potential.	'Bumph has its value'.
	C. Plan Calls	1. Customer Needs and Attitudes. 2. Products stocked/sited. 3. Competitors. 4. Equipment available.	1. Ability to indentify customer needs.	'Planned Calls are more effective than a cosy chat'.
	D. Make Effective Sales Presentation	1. Product Knowledge. 2. Customer Needs. 3. Sales Techniques. 4. Objection Handling. 5. Closing Techniques.	1. Open Interview. 2. Create Interest. 3. Present Benefits. 4. Overcome Objections. 5. Close Positively.	'Effective Selling is essential for success'.
	E. Involve Management when necessary.	1. Limitation of own Authority. 2. Price Limitations	1. Recognition of Need for Support.	'Many Hands make Light Work'.
2. TO FOSTER AND DEVELOP INDIVIDUAL PERSONAL RELATIONSHIPS WITH BEER CO. REPRESEN-TATIVES IN ORDER TO INDENTIFY AND EXPLOIT MUTUAL OPPORTUNITIES.	A. Contact with Beer Co. Representatives	1. Who are the Contacts. 2. Where they operate. 3. Who they know. 4. Beer Product Knowledge. 5. Customer Knowledge.	1. Establish mutual respect. 2. Sell Self. 3. Establish mutual benefits. 4. Identify customer/Group needs.	'We need all of the Salesmen we can get'

Figure 6.5 Wine trade salesperson's job description and job specification —*continued*

ITEM	TASK	KNOWLEDGE	SKILL	ATTITUDE
	B. Maintain contact to mutual advantage.	1. Who are the Contacts. 2. Where they operate. 3. Who they know. 4. Beer Product Knowledge. 5. Customer Knowledge.	1. Work together to mutual benefits. 2. Develop Action Plan.	'You scratch my back and I'll scratch yours'.
3. TO RECOMMEND AND AGREE A SALES ACTIVITY PLAN INCLUDING PROMOTIONAL MONIES AND LOAN EXPENDITURE WHICH WILL ENSURE THE ACHIEVEMENT OF THE SET TERRITORY OBJECTIVES.	A. Identify Prospects.	1. No. of Accounts. 2. Volume. 3. Location. 4. Present Situation. 5. Future Potential.	1. Ability to Select Priorities. 2. Good Admin.	'Time, effort and thought spent on planning'.
	B. Draw up Action Plan.	1. Company Activities. 2. Competitor Activity. 3. Timing. 4. Management Help Available. 5. Own Time Available.	1. Good Communication with Customers and Clear Understanding of Competitors. 2. Ability to set Realistic Objectives in realistic timescale. 3. Ability to assess Financial implications of proposals to both WVL and customer.	'An agreed Action Plan makes success more likely'.
4. TO BE AWARE OF MARKET TRENDS, PRODUCTS AND PRODUCT DEVELOPMENTS AND TO UNDERSTAND THE IMPLICATIONS OF THESE FACTORS FOR HIS/HER TERRITORY.	A. Read Trade Press.	1. Knowledge of Competitors and Potential Customers.	1. Self Train. 2. Learn and Apply. 3. Interpret Information. 4. Use Initiative.	'Learning is not a Classroom Operation'.
	B. Attend relevant Meetings and Events.	1. Trade Knowledge.	1. To listen and absorb objectively.	'Effective action depends on accurate and balanced reporting'.

Figure 6.5 Wine trade salesperson's job description and job specification — *continued*

ITEM	TASK	KNOWLEDGE	SKILL	ATTITUDE
	C. Assess Product Training Needs.	1. Conversant with Price List and Product Manual. 2. Knowledge of New Products.	1. Assimilate information and use to advantage.	'Good training is self inspired continuous and accumulative'.
5. TO PLAN AND ORGANISE CALL COVERAGE WHICH WILL ENABLE TELESALES PERSONNEL TO PROVIDE EFFECTIVE AND COMPLEMENTARY SALES CONTACT.	A. Motivate customers to take advantage of Tele-sales.	1. Customers Needs. 2. Customer Attitude.	1. Ability to identify Customer needs. 2. Ability to change Customer attitude.	'Effective Telesales use will give me more time to "SELL".'
	B. Plan, Call Coverage.	1. Telesales call timing/day. 2. Full relevant customer info. 3. Communication of Objectives.	1. Telesales call to complement Journey Plan. 2. Ability to identify customer needs.	'Effective Telesales use will give me more time to "SELL".'
6. TO SELL AND PROMOTE WVL AND PROP. BRANDS IN ORDER TO ACHIEVE TERRITORY MIX AND DISTRIBUTION OBJECTIVES.	A. Identify opportunities for Own brands.	1. Knowledge of brands currently stocked by customer. 2. What potential volumes are for Own Brands.	1. Ability to read stats. 2. Questioning technique to gain information. 3. Record information for future use.	'By knowing my customers business I am better able to advise him'.
	B. Product Knowledge.	1. Own Brands. 2. Competitors' brands. 3. Market trends.	1. Select particular benefits of product applicable to customer. 2. Use of strengths and weakness of competition. 3. Interpret changes in market and what opportunities.	'Good Product knowledge will help me overcome objections'.

Figure 6.5 Wine trade salesperson's job description and job specification —continued

ITEM	TASK	KNOWLEDGE	SKILL	ATTITUDE
	C. Draw Up Call Plan.	1. Brand Priorities. 2. Timing Presentation. 3. Volume/Discount Incentives to be offered. 4. Management Help Available. 5. Promotional Support Available. 6. Cost of WVL Concessions.	1. Interpreting sales targets. 2. Getting appointments. 3. Assess likely volume and recommend appropriate discount. 4. Deciding most appropriate form of support for product. 5. Select most appropriate product.	'With an overall plan for each call setting and achieving objectives is made easier'.
	D. Make effective Sales Presentation.	1. Customer Needs. 2. Presentation Techniques. 3. Objection Handling. 4. Negotiation Techniques. 5. Closing Techniques. 6. Sales Aids, samples, equipment and POS.	1. Open Interview. 2. Create Interest. 3. Present benefits. 4. Overcome Objections. 5. Use Sales Aids, samples, equipment and POS. 6. Close positively. 7. To negotiate commercially viable terms.	'Effective Selling and Negotiation is essential for success'.
7. TO ENSURE ALL WINE EQUIPMENT ACHIEVES TARGET VOLUME THROUGHPUT AND WHERE NECESSARY IS RE-SITED TO REALISE THIS	A. Monitor Wine volumes against Company criteria	1. Where equipment is sited. 2. What Company criteria is.	1. Interpret Sales Stats. 2. Identify accounts where maximum sales can be gained.	'All equipment must earn its keep'.
	B. Take remedial action.	1. Cause of low throughput. 2. Where to re-site	1. Questioning of customer to determine reasons of low throughput. 2. Making a persuasive case to customer for re-siting. 3. Maintaining agreed revised throughput.	

Figure 6.5 Wine trade salesperson's job description and job specification—*continued*

ITEM	TASK	KNOWLEDGE	SKILL	ATTITUDE
8. TO DEVELOP RELATIONSHIP WITH PEERS, SALES MANAGEMENT AND ALL RELATED DEPARTMENTS TO ENSURE THE COMMUNICATION OF MUTUALLY RELEVANT INFORMATION.	A. Established contact with related Departments eg. Marketing, Distribution, Finance, National Accounts, RTS.	1. Who are they? 2. What is their function? 3. Where are they located? 4. When can they be contacted? 5. What information/ assistance do they need?	1. Establish mutual contact. 2. Understand their function and how it affects you and your customers. 3. Establish own credibility. 4. Supply relevant facts required. 5. Work with them to mutual benefit.	'Its in all our interests to ensure good service to customers'
	B. Develop relationship with peers eg. Telesales, Key Account Manager.	1. Who are they? 2. What geographical areas do they cover? 3. What advice and assistance can they give?	1. Establish mutual contact and respect. 2. Explore areas, such as promotion evenings where you could work together. 3. Foster team spirit.	'Let's pull our knowledge and skills to mutual benefit'.
	C. Develop relationship with Area Sales Manager and Regional Sales Manager in own Region.	1. Who are they? 2. What are their responsibilities? 3. Where and when can they be contacted? 4. What advice/assistance can they give? 5. What reports and information do they require?	1. Establish mutual contact. 2. Understand their responsibilities. 3. Use their experience and skills. To develop own skills and further business. 4. Report accurately and on time as required.	'If we work as a team we stand a better chance of succeeding'.

Figure 6.5 Wine trade salesperson's job description and job specification—*continued*

ITEM	TASK	KNOWLEDGE	SKILL	ATTITUDE
9. TO MAINTAIN A COST EFFECTIVE CONTROL OVER PERSONAL EXPENSES AND TO REPORT DETAILS OF ENTERTAINMENT, TRAVELLING AND OTHER EXPENDITURE ACCURATELY AND REGULARLY AS REQUIRED BY MANAGEMENT.	A. Monitor accurately, all expenditure on a daily basis.	1. To be aware of perameters of maximum spend by segment. 2. All company documentation relating to personal expenditure.	1. To identify areas of spend to ensure maximum/profitable return. 2. To record/complete all documentation accurately and on time.	'Treat Company money with respect'. 'Integrity'.
10. TO MAINTAIN ALL ALLOCATED COMPANY EQUIPMENT, INCLUDING CAR, IN A CLEAN AND SERVICEABLE CONDITION AT ALL TIMES. TO ENSURE THAT SALES KIT AND PRESENTERS ARE UP-TO DATE AS WELL AS PROPERLY MAINTAINED.	A. Ensure Company Car is cleaned weekly, and serviced as per Company Policy.	1. Service intervals. 2. General car care?		'Remember, your car ALSO represents the Company AND IS an extension of your office'.
	B. To drive Company vehicle economically and with safety in mind at all times.	1. Laws, by-laws, Highway Code and ALSO Company Policy regarding drinking and driving.	1. Interpreting driving conditions sensibly at all times.	'Drive defensively at all times'.
	C. Ensure that sales kit/presenters accurately project the Company message.	1. Current Company products, prices, discount structures and promotional activity.	1. To make best use of visual aids to create maximum interest and customer awareness.	'A picture paints a thousand words'.
11. TO BE AVAILABLE TO WORK SUCH HOURS AS REQUIRED BY THE COMPANY.	A. To record a monthly ongoing itinerary and copy in relevant Management.	1. Geography equated to time.	1. Being able to plan with flexibility in mind.	'To make effective use of time, there should be no limits'.

Figure 6.5 Wine trade salesperson's job description and job specification —*concluded*

93

SELLING SALES TRAINING PLANS

The priorities decided, the field sales manager is faced with two challenges to his selling skills: selling and agreeing these priorities with management and agreeing the training objectives, and selling the training plans to those who will be trained through their implementation.

It is one of the ironies of commercial life that salespeople are trained to persuade customers to overcome their objections and to buy their company's products, services, or ideas. Yet all too infrequently are these skills put to work inside the company to sell ideas to colleagues, plans to senior management, or good training to salespeople.

Therefore field sales managers should prepare their respective sales meetings in advance, basing them upon the needs of senior management and the sales force, then sell these people training as they would sell to any other customer, remembering how 'buyers' buy and what is the sequence of their reaction: 'We are important and want to be respected'; 'Consider our needs'; 'How will your ideas help us?'; 'What are the facts?'; 'What are the snags?'; 'What shall we do?'; 'We approve'.

Action planning checklist

	Answers	Action and timing
1 Have the sales training needs of the categories of selling jobs been analysed?		
2 Have all the areas of knowledge, skills and attitudes been defined?		
3 Does the company have clearly defined sales performance standards against which to measure the effectiveness of field training?		
4 Has the company defined the training priorities for the next financial year?		

7:

Effective Learning and Communication

Learning depends upon a real connection between what is taught and the needs of those people who are being taught. The field sales manager must keep this principle firmly in mind if he is to train, develop and motivate his salespeople to achieve the sales results they both want.

In looking at the processes of learning and communication and applying them to how to train salespeople effectively, a direct parallel can be drawn with the selling role itself. Selling, after all, can as easily and as accurately be described as *teaching customers how to satisfy their needs*. The following are then true of salesmen and training them:

1   As a trainer the field sales manager is the salesman selling the benefits of his ideas to his customers: the salesmen, to meet and satisfy their needs.
2   The field sales manager should practise in training salespeople the same techniques he asks and develops the salespeople to apply in selling to customers.
3   As a trainer the field sales manager is selling the benefits that will be enjoyed by the salesman from changes in behaviour and technique.
4   The manager has made a 'sale' when learning has taken place.
5   Until the changes needed have taken place the manager has not sold his ideas or achieved his training objectives.
6   If the changes in behaviour do not occur then it is due to shortcomings in the manager's knowledge, skill and training ability, not the (customer's) salesman's fault.

These factors underline the need for the field sales manager to understand how learning takes place and how this process is linked to the quality of the communications between the manager and the salesman.

WHAT DO WE MEAN BY COMMUNICATION?

A field sales manager does not have to be an expert in psychology to be an effective trainer. What he does need to be able to do competently is to apply the basic principles of learning and communication to developing the selling skills of his salesmen.

First, how does learning take place? The learning process is dependent upon our human communication mechanisms, so the problem of learning new skills is basically a problem of communication. In simple terms, we communicate with one another through the senses. Communication can be said to take place when an identical message in the mind of one person is transferred to the mind of another. This rarely happens, for a variety of reasons we will explore later. Since communication is the basic ingredient affecting people's ability to learn, let us examine the objectives of communications, the barriers to effective communication and how they can be overcome.

COMMUNICATIONS OBJECTIVES

The field sales manager's ultimate success depends upon his ability to communicate persuasively with his salespeople so that they will achieve through their efforts the planned sales objectives he has set them. His five communication objectives are to ensure that his salespeople: *hear* what he tells them (or sees what he shows them), *understand* what they hear or see, *agree,* and take *action.* The manager will only know if he is achieving these four communication objectives if he receives *feedback* from his listeners of what they have heard, how much of it they have understood, to what extent they agree or disagree and whether they are prepared to take the required action, some other action, or do nothing. This all sounds so easy and simple, but every reader will have his own stories to add to the endless library of failures in communication. Some examples of failures in communication are shown in Figure 7:1.

	Message sent by communicator	Message received or reply given by receiver
1	Please write down answer to question: 'Where are elephants found?'	An 11 plus examination candidate wrote: 'Because they are so large they are seldom lost'
2	Can I watch the Eclipse this afternoon on your television? (Meant the Eclipse Stakes at Newmarket, a horse race)	'I can do better than that for you – here is a piece of smoked glass'
3	A pharmaceutical salesman promoting a product to alleviate pain after bruises are inflicted, said: 'This gets right into the bone, doctor'	The doctor asked: 'How does the patient get it out afterwards?'
4	A housewife in Chelmsford, England, asked an oil company representative to call because her domestic heating system had broken down. A call was made by the oil company salesman in company with a technical fuel oil adviser. Contamination of the oil by water was suspected. Within the hearing of the housewife the salesman asked the technical adviser to 'fetch a thief from the Chelmsford depot as quickly as you can' (A thief is the technical name for a device for taking samples of oil)	The housewife replied: 'I would rather you didn't. I have been burgled once already this year and after the recent escape I feel very nervous'. The housewife referred to the escape of a prisoner from Chelmsford gaol just a few days before this conversation took place. To her the word 'thief' had only one meaning.

Figure 7.1 Some examples of communication failures

WHAT ARE THE BARRIERS TO EFFECTIVE COMMUNICATION?

Salespeople cannot learn efficiently until the manager commences teaching, that is to say, communicating ideas, skills, and reasons for change. Thus the onus for success or failure in getting the message heard, understood, agreed with and acted upon rests with the manager, not his salespeople. Likewise, when selling, the onus for getting through to the customer rests with the salespeople. A number of difficulties arise to prevent the communicator achieving his five communication objectives:

- *Communication objective: to hear* (or see). People cannot concentrate for long periods on either the spoken (or written) word. They pay less attention to what is unimportant to them – what does not help them or concern their needs.
- *Communication objective: to understand.* People misunderstand more easily what they hear but do not see. They make assumptions based upon their past experience which colours what they have heard. People do not always understand the specialised language (trade jargon). People often draw conclusions before hearing the whole communication.
- *Communication objective: to agree.* People do not like being proved wrong, or being told that which conflicts with their own value standards or previous experience, and are often suspicious of those with an interest in changing their minds.
- *Communication objective: to act.* People fear the results of taking wrong decisions. They do not easily change their habits. This is very noticeable when older untrained salespeople undergo sales training even when what they were doing was ineffective.
- *Communication objective: feedback.* The relationship between a manager and a salesman makes frank exchanges difficult. People tend to deliberately hide what they really think and tell the manager what they think he would like (rather than what he needs) to hear. Also, appearances can be deceptive. A nod may not always indicate understanding. It might mask ignorance or indecision.

These difficulties are common to manager and salesman, salesman and customer, and to the majority of human beings.

If we examine the human communications process we can better understand how it works, how the failures in communication arise, and what we can do to be more effective.

How we communicate can be compared with a radio transmitter and receiver (see Figure 7:2). Messages are received through our senses; we then form impressions and assimilate or associate them with other information and ideas stored in the brain. Before we respond to what has been communicated, the brain reacts in the following sequence to this new information:

- It scans existing memories of past experiences and finds the frame of reference or memory which relates most closely to the new information.
- The new information is sent to join the existing memory or frame of reference chosen.
- If it is associated with what that memory perceived, the new information is analysed and subsequently fitted into the existing memory pattern.

As a result of this filing system of the brain, the existing memory may:

1   Remain the same but stronger
2   Change for the better
3   Change for the worse

We can all recall examples of the results of this memory bank at work. The customer who, having tried a product which failed to live up to its claims, refuses to listen to a salesman who quite genuinely tells him that modifications have completely cured the fault. The salesman who responds enthusiastically to the manager's sales-training field visits because, having rather

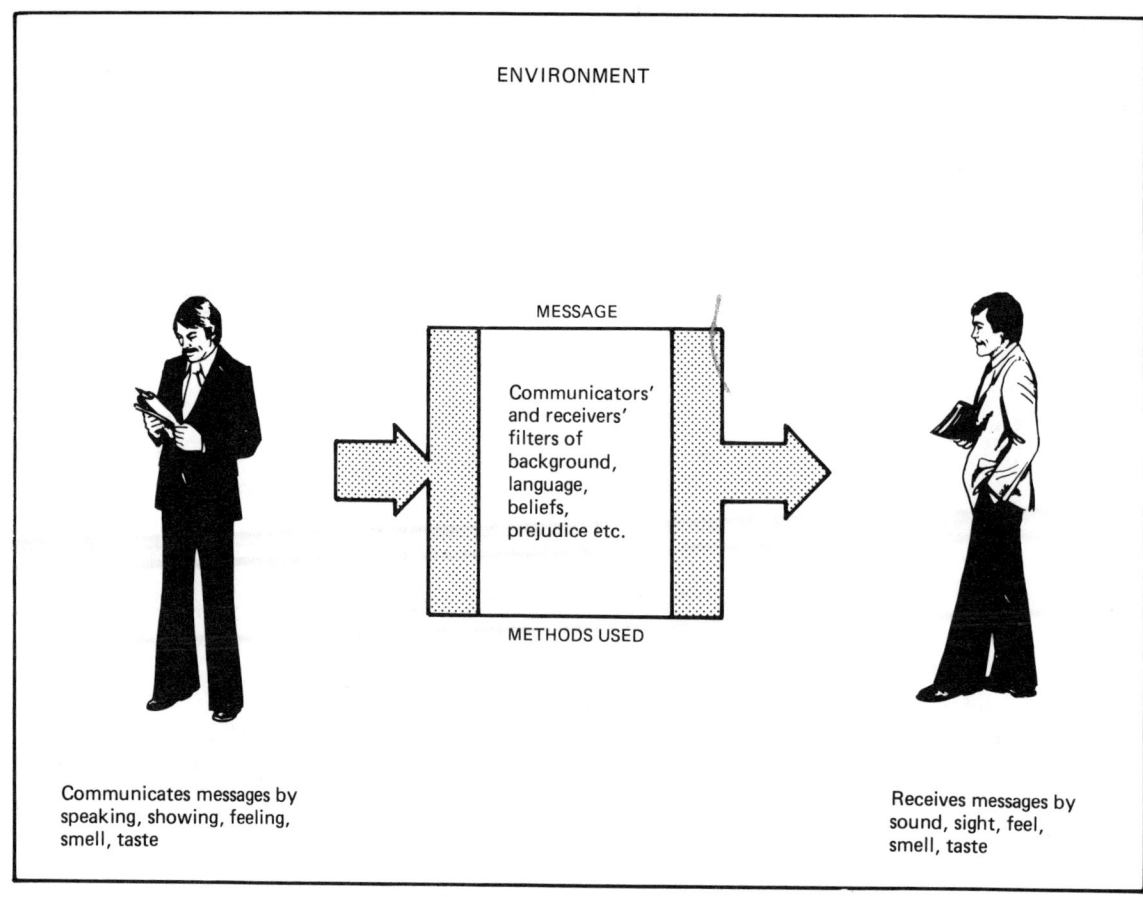

ENVIRONMENT

MESSAGE

Communicators' and receivers' filters of background, language, beliefs, prejudice etc.

METHODS USED

Communicates messages by speaking, showing, feeling, smell, taste

Receives messages by sound, sight, feel, smell, taste

Figure 7.2 How the human communication system operates

doubtfully applied the techniques he was first taught, found they worked for him time and again.

Other factors influence the quality of our communications, such as the value standards of the communicator and listener, the message being transmitted, the filters through which the message passes, the methods of communication used, and the environment in which the communication takes place.

The value standards of communicator and listener

Our backgrounds, education, beliefs, ethical standards and prejudices, all affect the way we communicate with one another. Thus two people looking at the same object or listening to the same story may perceive and react to it in quite different ways. In training situations where such differences exist, it is vital for the field sales manager to try and perceive things through the eyes of his salesmen. It will be by association of his ideas and experiences that the manager will be able to communicate with him.

The message being transmitted

The same words mean different things to different people. Add to this the jargon that has crept into the language of business and the result is confusion.

The filters through which the message passes

Because each person thinks more often than not about himself than about the person he is communicating with, his words and what he says reflect this. His own words, prejudices, beliefs and jargon, can set up filters which confuse the message sent and received.

The methods of communication used

No two people hear, see and feel with equal efficiency. Some you can tell and they understand immediately. Others have to be told, shown and asked to play back their understanding before a message gets through. For this reason when communicating ideas a manager should always involve at least two senses. Thus a sales objective cannot only be discussed verbally; it can also be more firmly fixed in the minds of both manager and salesman if it is written down.

The environment in which communication takes place

The relationship between the manager and a salesman is a business one in which the former has influence over the career, development and success of the latter. These factors condition the environment in which they work and communicate with each other. Thus unless he is very unusual (or financially independent), a salesman in a training situation in the field will tend to tailor his words to the manager's efforts. He may think very different thoughts from what he actually says. This is why it is so vital for the manager to create an atmosphere of trust and confidence when training. *Training* and *censorship* must be totally divorced from one another to enable the salesman to be himself and speak his mind.

These are the five main barriers to effective communication and learning in the field training situation in which the manager seeks to develop his salesmen through his words and actions.

HOW LEARNING TAKES PLACE

A basic understanding of the communication process is essential to understanding the learning process. Now let us return to how learning takes place. Learning takes place as a result of relating new information to past experience. This new information will then add to or modify the store of experience and influence future responses. Thus every experience, every new piece of information, every sales interview contributes to what we know, feel or believe now. It influences our reactions to any new information in the future.

Learning is progressively influenced by past experience.

A change in the selling performance of a salesman therefore requires a change to take place in the mind of the salesman.

WHAT INFLUENCES SELLING PERFORMANCE?

In training salesmen the manager seeks to influence and improve sales performance. Performance can be described as the result of a mixture of knowledge, attitudes, skills and ability. Similarly, how we learn affects or is affected by our knowledge, by our attitudes and by our skills.

When applying his knowledge of how people learn the practical task of training salespeople the field sales manager should remember four things:

1   Training should always be closely related to the salesman's past experience. This emphasises the importance of the field sales manager learning as much as he can about a man's background at the selection interview before he joins a company. This knowledge will help the manager to get on the same 'wave-length' as his salespeople.

2   Individuals learn at different speeds. Training should be paced to the salesman's ability to understand and retain knowledge. Too much information in too short a time can clog up the communication process and make a mess of the man's filing system. The individual 'curve of learning' is like the classic race between the hare and the tortoise. Some people tear away with an initial spurt of learning but then seem to lose concentration and tail off: others, like the tortoise, begin slowly but then gather speed and learn effectively and become steady reliable performers.

3   Training should always reinforce learning. In the communication process people obtain a body of knowledge by receiving messages from all the senses. Thus someone who has been taught to drive a car by a trained instructor and passes his driving test will subsequently be influenced to drive carefully or carelessly by a number of subsequent pieces of information received through the senses, e.g. causing a crash through being late for an appointment, followed by seeing a warning on television about the number of accidents caused by motorists not planning their journeys to allow plenty of time to get there, followed by a talk from the field sales manager about allowing at least 15 minutes between appointments in case of delays, can all add up to a change in behaviour based upon learning and modifying information. Relating this to training, the manager needs to use several methods for reinforcing learning: by telling the salesman the same thing in different ways, or by asking the salesman questions, the answers to which will draw out their comprehension of what they have been told.

4   Because selling is a social skill used to persuade and influence customers, managers must not overlook the influence customers can and do have on salesmen. One sure sign that a salesman has never had any training or field supervision is that he speaks and sounds more like a customer!

Training, then, should provide a means of continual revision and practice of the right answers or methods to develop and fix knowledge and selling skills, e.g. in situations where salespeople face frequent rejection such as those selling speciality products, services, insurance, the first skill to crack (and quickly) is closing the sale. Salespeople decide that since asking for the order courts refusal and is uncomfortable, they stop asking for the order. The result is comfort for the salesman in his relationship with the customer, but no commission. In one company such rejection is very high. The pioneer salesmen make 60 selling calls a week and on average the best salesmen are only successful in three calls. The field sales management has therefore got to be highly supportive and the training to rebuild and fix selling technique and confidence must be frequent. Each salesman has a field training visit by his field sales manager every five working days plus telephone conversations every day.

DIFFERENCES IN PERSPECTIVE OF MANAGER AND SALESMAN

The field sales manager must always take account of the differences between his job and his perspective of selling, his experience and environment and that of his salespeople. Even more contrasting will be the perspective of head office staff who communicate with the salesmen. Some of these differences between manager and salesmen are listed in Figure 7:3.

These differences do not help the training task of the field sales manager, but they do underline the need to resolve them and plan training from the salesman's point in terms of his needs, his problems, and how he sees the products and services the company asks him to sell.

The nature of the sales job and the mechanisms by which people learn present a paradox which the field sales manager must resolve. Sales training is directed towards equipping the salesman to tackle *future* customer relationships persuasively and successfully to achieve *future* company objectives. Learning which should be the result of good sales training is linked to *past* experience and must match and be compatible with the salesman's personal objectives.

Salesman	Field Sales Manager
1 Spends the bulk of his time with customers	1 Is more closely involved with the company as well as with the customers
2 Gets the bulk of his information from customers	2 Belief in the company and its products is not being constantly questioned by customers
3 Has a lonely job cut off from other company staff	3 Is employed to get results through the efforts of others and not to get them himself
4 Has to live with the social tensions of the sales situation every day	4 Is employed to improve other people's performance
5 Has to live with rejections and some failures	5 Is usually a good and experienced salesman himself, so unlike the new salesman in particular, he knows what happens and why and so understands how to do it
6 Needs to be liked by and to get approval from customers	6 Can remember sales successes and forget failures because his failures are in the past and not facing him every day. The danger that comes from this is a belief that selling is easy all the time
	7 Has more frequent contact with the company and can draw support from it

Figure 7.3 Perspective and environment differences between the salesman and field sales manager

This brings us right back to the relationship between the training job and the selling job the field sales manager has to carry out to succeed. His salespeople are his *customers*. As a trainer he must sell them the benefits of his learning, using sound proven selling techniques. He must therefore plan his training in terms of the *needs* of his salespeople and how they can be met (see the Action Planning Checklist).

Action planning checklist

	Answers	Action and timing
1 What are the needs of the salesman?		
2 How does he see his problems?		
3 How can training be sold to him?		
4 What is my training objective?		
5 How can these training objectives be made into learning objectives?		
6 How can his past experience be used to assist learning?		
7 How can his early success be ensured?		
8 How can I minimise his mistakes?		
9 How can I reinforce learning with successful results?		
10 How can I guard against being a stimulating manager but a mediocre trainer?		
11 How can I eliminate weaknesses by building on his strengths?		

8: Field Training Methods and Techniques

Before any field training can be carried out, the field sales manager must first decide what training objectives should be set, what training methods will be most apropriate and how the results of the training will be measured.

WHAT TRAINING OBJECTIVES SHOULD BE SET?

Having identified a salesman's individual training needs and matched them to the company's needs, specific training objectives should be set to enable the field sales manager to concentrate his time and skill and to harness the motivation of the trainee. The criteria of good sales training objectives are that they should describe:

1 What the trainee should be able to do at the end of the training.
2 The conditions under which he should be able to do it.
3 The standards of performance he should be able to achieve.

HOW TO SET TRAINING OBJECTIVES

The field sales manager's sales training plans must be set in measurable terms in three main areas: the overall objective of the proposed sales training in terms of its contribution to the company's total or specific marketing objectives, its specific objective and the methods to be used, and the individual objectives of training related to the job performance of each salesman.

An example of how these training objectives might be set out for a specific sales situation is now given.

A company plans to launch a new product on 1 May. The product is higher priced and available in larger packs than existing products. This creates a training need for the sales force as a whole, the need to specify the means of carrying out stages of training for the sales force, and the relation of both to the needs of individuals. The training objectives in the three areas might be set out as follows:

1 *Overall objectives.* It is intended that as a result of training completed by 14 April the sales force will:
   (a) Possess the new knowledge and skills necessary to enable them to sell the new product.
   (b) Be able to demonstrate their ability to use this knowledge and skill in category A and B outlets.
   (c) Be able to achieve the agreed standards of order size, pack size sold and unit price.
2 *Method objectives.* Training will be carried out by means of:
   (a) Formal presentation of plans by sales and marketing management. The objective is to ensure that the sales force receives full information on the new product, full details of the launch programme, and is motivated to want to sell the new product.
   (b) Regional sales training meetings. The objective of the meetings is to ensure that the sales force understands the information given, knows how to use it in selling the new product, and demonstrates skill during role-playing.
   (c) Field accompaniment. The objective of this is to ensure that the sales force can demonstrate their ability on the job and are able to achieve the agreed standards of performance.
3 *Individual objectives.* Specific additional training objectives for a salesman who has, say, been identified as needing particular training in overcoming price objections. At the end of the field accompaniment the salesman should:
   (a) Know the company's six prescribed methods of answering price objections.
   (b) Be able to demonstrate his ability to use the six methods when selling the new high priced product to both existing and prospective customers.
   (c) Be able to achieve the standards of order size, pack size and price per unit agreed for the new product.

Selling is a social skill and essentially sales training should be aimed at improving the effectiveness of the salesman's communication in face-to-face meetings with customers. The purpose of setting clear and specific sales training objectives is therefore to ensure that those being trained know how to use the knowledge and skills they are taught, that they are able to demonstrate effective use of the knowledge and skills, and are able to achieve agreed standards of performance as a result.

WHICH TRAINING METHOD TO USE IN FIELD TRAINING

When planning the individual training of a salesman, the principles of learning and their application should be remembered, particularly the following:

1 Relevance to past experience is essential for everyone in learning of new information before they can accept it and then apply it. This was emphasised in the chapter on effective learning and communication, pages 97–99.
2 Research has shown that what people only *hear* and do not *see* they forget quickly. The speed at which they forget places a major question mark against the gaps between some managers' field training visits particularly if no note was taken of the important points that were made on the last visit and you only have your memory to remind you! People forget 38% of what they have been told only after 2 days; 65% after 8 days and no less than 75% after 30 days.

3 Salesmen can only develop usable skills by applying what they have learnt on the job.
4 Research has repeatedly shown in the classroom and when accompanying salesmen on the job that knowledge is retained for much longer and selling skills are developed faster when the following five step formula is used:

1. *Tell* the salesman what to do

> e.g.   – planning his week's work
> – planning a call
> – analysing a customer's needs

2. *Show* the salesman how to do it.

> e.g.   – the manager demonstrates how he plans a call
> – the manager takes a selling call to demonstrate how selling techniques are translated into real life.

3. Get the salesman to *practice* what he has been told and shown,

> e.g.   – get the salesman to plan a call
> get the salesman to carry out a selling call
> based on what he has planned.

4. *Assess* what the salesman did and *correct/coach* where necesssary.

> e.g.   – measure his call against how he planned to carry it out and highlight the differences and the results and show him how to improve.

5. Get him to *practise AGAIN* and *AGAIN* and *AGAIN*
until you and he are sure that he has mastered the product knowledge, planning technique or selling skill you set out to help him develop.

METHODS OF TRAINING

These principles provide guidelines in the selection of the five main training methods and techniques the field sales manager can use to develop skills on the job. These are: demonstration, role playing, coaching using the ten steps in field sales training technique, product knowledge by programmed learning, and the sales manual.

Demonstration

The demonstration method of training is where the field sales manager plans and carries out a real selling call on a customer or prospect with the salesman he is training present as a silent observer. This method is most appropriately used when training a new salesman.

Here it is imperative that the manager, through the calls he conducts, achieves two training objectives. First, he demonstrates the level of selling skill he wants the new salesman to *reach* and *exceed*; and secondly, in doing so he establishes his own competence in the eyes of the new man. Sales managers often express reservations about this method of training and question its effectiveness. After all, the number of footballers, golfers, cricketers and other sportsmen who watch their heroes each weekend are legion, but the competition at the top does not exactly become unsupportable!

A number of studies have shown that demonstration can teach as well as, or better than, observing in a classroom if certain conditions are fulfilled by the manager. For instance, before the demonstration call takes place, the salesman should be taken through each stage of the call so that he fully understands what the manager is going to do and how he is going to do it.

The salesman will learn more if before the call takes place he is directed to concentrate his attention on a particular aspect of the demonstration. Tests have repeatedly shown that when a 'role-played' call is carried out in the classroom and recorded on closed-circuit television, observing salesmen are much more helpful in the analysis of a colleague's performance if they are asked to watch only *one* part of the sale and write down their thoughts on a structured evaluation form.

A fundamental and most essential condition is that the salesman must respect the manager carrying out the demonstration and believe that he is a successful salesman. The implications that flow from meeting this condition are considerable. It means that if a manager is training by demonstration he must be able to sell. Being successful does not mean being a star performer. In fact, few star salesmen make good trainers because they rarely understand what makes them star salesmen and so cannot communicate how it is done to others. Successful means setting a demanding above-average standard which if imitated will enable the salesman to achieve at *least* a competent level of salesmanship.

Role playing

In role playing, the salesman and the field sales manager try out the respective roles of the customer and the salesman away from the real sales situation. This is done either before the call is about to be made, to rehearse the whole or a part of the call, or afterwards, to improve a selling technique which was faulty in the call. Role-playing sessions conducted on the job by the manager are the most effective because feedback is almost immediate from the success or failure of the subsequent call. The manager must use his judgement as to the wisdom of role playing the entire call or only a particular part of it and the selling technique that will be involved at that stage. Role playing can form part of a comprehensive 'ten step' coaching technique which will be examined later in this chapter. To be successful the role-playing technique has to be conducted with great skill. The following conditions will contribute to developing selling skill through role playing:

1   Use 'live ammunition'. Role playing carried out on the job should be designed to improve how a salesman conducts an actual customer call, so that the call plan provides the actual material.

2   The call, or the part of it to be role played, should be prepared carefully. The salesman should be asked what aspect of a particular call he has found difficult so that what is practised will produce the most effective results in the call when it is carried out, e.g. the opening, the presentation, using visual aids, getting the customer to talk, handling objections, closing, etc.

3   Reversing roles. It can help the salesman to develop a better understanding of the needs, motives and problems of the customer he is about to sell to if he first role plays the part of the customer and the manager takes the part of the salesman. It will develop his understanding of the customer's situation. To illustrate this, just a simple question by the field sales manager such as: 'Harry, put yourself into the customer's position. You are the managing director, Mr Head, facing this problem, how would you react?', will enhance the salesman's comprehension of the attitude and mind of the buyer. (Those who want to study this very productive approach to selling further should read the article 'Behavioural Approach to Industrial Selling' by J. W. Thompson and W. W. Evans in the *Harvard Business Review,* March – April 1969 edition.) After reversing roles the manager should question the salesman and summarise the lessons learned and then role play the situation a second time, but with the salesman playing his own role as the salesman and the manager this time the part of the customer.

4   Use a portable tape recorder to play back to the salesman the role-playing situation he

Steps	Objective	Steps	Objective
	Before each call		*During the call*
Step 1	*Analyses customer record card*	*Step 5*	*Watch and listen*
	When was last call made?		Look at the salesman not the customer
	Which products were presented?		Avoid unplanned intervention
	What objections were raised?		Look for changes from the agreed plan
	Which products were sold?		What were the reasons for them?
	Which were not sold?		What effect did they have on the outcome of the call?
	What information was obtained?		Is the commercial situation as the salesman described?
			Is the call objective(s) achieved?
Step 2	*Help salesman plan and prepare the call*		What weaknesses are there in his presentation?
	What are the call objectives?		What improvements since last call?
	What are the customer's needs?		What is being done well?
	What products are to be presented and in what order?		*After the call*
	How will the call be opened?	*Step 6*	*Analyse salesman's performance in call. Follow a sequence: 'Kerbside conference'*
	What sales aids will be used?		First praise in detail all things well done
	Which benefits will be mentioned and in what order?		Question salesman to get him to identify weaknesses – if there were any
	What facts will be used to support and prove these benefits?		If he does not recognise them help him to see them.
	What questions will be asked to check customer's agreement?		Agree them with him
	What are the likely objections and how will they be handled?		Show him how to correct weakness by practice or demonstration
	How will the call be closed?	*Step 7*	*Assist salesman in completing customer record card*
Step 3	*Ensure salesman understands and agrees the call plan*		Set an example by ensuring this is done immediately after the call and sell the benefits of doing this of accurate information useful for the next call on this customer.
	If necessary rehearse any aspects of the call – the opening or closing techniques or how a particular objection will be answered	*Step 8*	*Set specific objectives for the next call on this customer*
		Step 9	*Make sure these objectives are recorded by the salesman*
Step 4	*Agree what part manager will take in call*		The salesman is likely to be alone on his next call on this customer
	Tell the salesman if the manager will observe the whole call or deal with just a specific part. If only a part agree with him what it will be. Remember the dangers of unplanned intervention.	*Step 10*	*Arrange and agree a specific time when improvement can be checked*
			Next call?
			Next day?
			Next week?
			The week after?

Figure 8.1 Ten steps in field sales training

has performed. Before making any comment about it himself, the manager should *always* first ask the salesman to comment on it. Such feedback has been found to sharpen people's perception of their own behaviour and to accelerate the acquisition of selling skill.

Coaching: ten steps in field-sales training

The ten steps field-sales training technique is the most comprehensive on-the-job method of training and also the most thorough. It incorporates a recognised sequence, in training people on an individual basis, of: *preparing* the salesman, explaining precisely *what* he should do, showing *how* it is to be done, *observing* him perform, and *evaluating* his performance and correcting it if necessary. These logical steps provide a method of coaching covering the preparation before a sales interview, the interview itself, and the evaluation of what happened after the sales interview. The ten-steps technique is illustrated in Figure 8:1.

By following these steps the field sales manager is able to marry his own management and selling skills to his training objectives. The ten steps apply to the field training plan, to the organisation of a day's sales work, and specifically to each call jointly made by the manager and salesman during training. When using it to develop selling skills, the call rate for the day in question *will* drop. More time will inevitably be taken to plan each call and in reviewing it afterwards. For these reasons the manager should conserve it for specially selected calls where it is necessary to bring about the maximum impact and improvement. For instance, for a local bank manager trying to obtain the deposit accounts of a solicitors' partnership handling large industrial conveyances in a town but who are currently banking with another bank. Or for a medical representative promoting an antibiotic and persuading a group practice of doctors known to be heavy prescribers of a competitor's product, but who for one reason or another are not at present prescribing the particular company's brand. Or for a representative of a northern port trying to persuade a major food supermarket group, bringing all its overseas deliveries into an East Anglian port, to transfer some shipments to the north.

The ten steps technique is as follows:

Before each call
Step one. The manager and salesman analyse the record card of the customer, or if there is no record card, the other collected information; they review when last call was made and what happened: which products or services were discussed, what business is the customer in or interested in, who does he buy from at present (if known) and why, etc.

Step two. The manager helps the salesman to set specific objectives for the call and to plan and prepare it in terms of the needs that will be explored, what products or services and their benefits will be discussed, and how the call will be opened, the presentation and objections handled, and the commitment that will be asked for and how it will be achieved.

Step three. The manager discusses the sales-call plan with the salesman so that both understand and know what is going to happen. At this step it is important that the manager checks whether the salesman is unsure about his ability to handle a particular part of the planned call effectively, e.g. a series of tricky objections which are anticipated, or a closing technique.

Step four. The manager then agrees with the salesman what role he will take in the call and how he will be introduced, or how they will introduce themselves if the customer is unknown to either of them. This is a most vital step and too often an interview plan has gone sour because the field sales manager could not resist the temptation to show off his prowess as a salesman, or wanted his status – rather than the salesman's – inflated, by insisting he be introduced as the man's manager. Obviously sometimes the fact that the manager is introduced as the senior member of the company can help the customer/salesman relationship, but let the salesman be the best judge of this.

During the call
Step five. The call having commenced, the manager should watch and listen. This is not easy for the field sales manager to do, probably having been a salesman. If the sales interview does not go according to plan or the prospect of a large order looks like slipping away through the salesman's inadequacy, the manager will be tempted to intervene and rescue the situation. If this was a joint-selling call, well and good, but it isn't. It is a *training call* and the objective is to improve how this and all the other, possibly 100 or more, calls the salesman will make *unobserved* during the rest of the month are handled. Furthermore, once the manager becomes involved in the to and fro of the discussion he can no longer be an impartial observer able to help the salesman after the call and analyse what happened. So within the bounds of good manners the manager's objective is to observe the progress of the sales interview, whether the salesman is successful in achieving the planned objective, and how persuasively he used selling technique.

After the call
Step six. Following the call, the manager usually will return to the car to discuss the call. This is a vital part of the salesman's training and the conversation that takes place at this stage has come to be known as the 'kerbside conference'. The discussion is based upon the psychology of persuasion and is structured to allow correction to take place if necessary, but in a way that is positive and not demoralising.

First the manager shows appreciation of any part of the call that was particularly well-handled. This praise opens the discussion on a favourable rather than a critical basis, but it must be sincere. Even if the call was badly handled there are usually one or two good parts the manager can identify that are worthy of comment.

Second, the manager asks the salesman to analyse the sales interview. This is worth doing, even if it was entirely successful, because by identifying the ingredients of that success they will reinforce the learning process. If it did not go well, the manager should not at this stage say so. The salesman may not have the same impression and to know that the manager says it was a disaster will inhibit further and frank discussion. To get the salesman talking it is better to say: 'Let us take out the call plan we prepared. Looking at the sales objective we agreed to go for, what did you think went well and what not so well?' If he cannot or will not himself identify the weaknesses in the interview that were within his power to control, then obviously he must be told, but skilfully, because the aim is to get *his* agreement so that some remedial action can be taken.

Third, once the weaknesses have been agreed upon the manager must carry out coaching to correct them. This may take the form of role playing the technique that was inadequate, or analysing the sales objections and working out answers that can be employed on the next meeting with the customer. The more participative this coaching is, and the more the manager can guide the salesman to find the solutions, the better.

Step seven. When coaching is over it is tempting to look at the time and drive on to the next call; but the kernel of the coaching must first be put in a safe place where it can be found and well used. Ask the salesman to complete the customer record card and help him in this by reminders of the salient points of the call and the lessons learned from the post-call analysis and coaching which will be employed next time. Also, sell the benefits of speedy and accurate completion of the record card. Too-little information or none-at-all, are not the bricks with which to build a bridge to the next sale. All they result in is a dogmatic, illogical sales presentation canned for anyone's consumption, rather than planned and based upon an individual customer's identified needs.

Step eight. Discuss the plans the salesman has in mind for the next call on this customer. Based upon the information entered on the record card, help him to set specific objectives for this call, and:

Step nine. Make sure these specific objectives are recorded by the salesman in writing either on the customer's record card or in a specific objectives book he keeps for the purpose. He will probably be alone when he next calls on this customer. The reminder of this need to have a specific objective for the call related to the customer's needs will help him to plan his call better.

Step ten. Arrange and agree a specific time when the improvement you have aimed to bring about on this training visit can be checked, e.g. on the next call on the customer or on the next day or the next week. This follow-up is like waiting for the results of an examination. If they get lost in the post and never arrive, there is disappointment and demotivation. The same will happen if you agree to check what happens and forget to do so. The fact that you cannot be physically with the salesman to make this check does not prevent you from making this follow up. Use the telephone. Call him on a particular evening, or at the end of the day on which he has made the return call on the customer, and ask him to tell you how he got on.

This ten step technique orchestrates every management and training skill and above all, puts to work the nub of what the field sales manager job is about: getting planned sales objectives achieved through the efforts of his salespeople.

It may not always be practical to carry out a thorough 'kerbside conference' after each selected call, where this method of training has been employed. Depending on circumstances, it may sometimes be better to set aside 15 minutes during the lunchtime break to review comprehensively the special call or calls you have made with the salesman.

The 'kerbside conference' will only be successful if the manager concentrates on identifying *technical* faults or deficiencies in performance, discusses them specifically and helps the salesman to improve upon them. Generalisations about the call by the manager such as: 'That went well. Now let's do it again at the next call' or 'You had better not do that again or you will never make a sale today', do not provide the salesman with any detailed insight into his performance. He needs to know what happened, however bad, so that he can repeat the good things done and avoid bad things. Another factor in the 'kerbside conference' is that it need not be a lengthy procedure. Indeed, the salesman's morale will take a serious dip if it is. The verbatim example given in Figure 10.3 only takes about four minutes. But do not even go through the motions of this exercise in a hurry just for the sake of following procedure. Such brevity will be purchased at the cost of accurate appraisal.

Product knowledge by programmed learning

However good a salesman's selling technique is, it must be backed by sound product knowledge learned from the customer's point of view. Whilst such knowledge can be absorbed to a limited extent by lectures, films and discussions, this is usually inadequate to ensure accurate retention. The salesman must be aware of the following:

1   What need inspired the creation of the product or service.
2   What it will do for the buyer or user.
3   What the product or service is.
4   Why it is made as it is.
5   How it works.
6   Its exclusive features and benefits.

7   What it costs and why it costs what it does.

8   What warranties stand behind it.

Such knowledge can be developed by means of programmed learning designed for use by the individual salesman in the work situation. The advantages are that the salesman can learn at his own rate, either at home or on the job, and the subject matter can usually be learned more thoroughly. Some companies prepare programmes on a written question and answer basis. Others equip their salesmen's cars with cassette players. The product knowledge related to each product is recorded on cassettes. Learning can then be achieved by the salesman playing these tapes as he drives along or between calls. The availability of both types makes it possible for the field sales manager to set precise product knowledge to be learned before a field visit and then to check it when he sees a salesman. Alternatively, at the end of one field training visit he can set as a training objective a specific area of product knowledge to be studied, and then make a short two-hour appointment with the salesman just to check whether he has learned it.

The sales manual

Another means of self-training is the sales manual. In some companies this document is only an administrative procedures manual but others have compiled one that really justifies the title workbook rather than manual. Apart from containing instructions on how to compile reports, write out invoices, and deal with payments and car expenses, it should be full of explicit guidelines on products, selling techniques and work organisation. In one engineering group the sales manual is so comprehensive that it provides all the material needed to furnish the new salesman with product knowledge and selling technique on his initial training course at headquarters. As each part of the course is completed, another section is added to his sales manual. It is looseleaf, with every page dated. When amendments are made, the relevant pages are removed and the replacements inserted. Such a manual becomes a source of constant reference for both the field sales manager and his salespeople. As with programmed learning, the manager can revise a section of the manual with the salesman before or after a call. It becomes a working tool and the manager must ensure by his constant references to it that his salesmen come to use it as a bible – studied daily.

HOW WILL THE RESULTS OF FIELD TRAINING BE MEASURED?

Field training and the individual development of each member of the sales force is the job of the field sales manager; but it takes time. The price of this investment must be measured by the return it yields from improved sales performance. Field training is therefore a part of the control which must be kept of the selling efforts within a company and so field training must itself be controlled.

The methods by which the manager reports on the regular visits to his staff, on what they do and how they do it, will be indicators of his performance as a manager. The four controls which influence the quantity and quality of the salesman's activities are:

1   *Who is called upon:* set in terms of categories of existing customers and potential customers and/or by customer profile.

2   *How many are called upon:* the numbers of customers and potential customers to be seen within a given period based upon a standard call-rate for customers and prospects.

3   *How often such customers and prospects are called on:* based upon the call frequency set for the satisfactory servicing and expansion of existing customers and the acquisition of new business from prospective customers.

4   *What is done in each call:* the quality of selling carried out based upon standards set by the field sales manager from field reports and appraisals.

These four controls, especially the last one, are the means by which the field sales manager measures the performance of his salesmen and the effectiveness of his training. An example of how these four controls are expressed in descriptive but measureable terms is illustrated in Figure 8.2.

Action planning checklist

	Answers	Action and timing
1 Does the company have precisely defined training objectives set for the sales force?		
2 Are the present methods and techniques of field training appropriate to ensure the effective development of the sales force? If not, what actions are necessary to equip the sales management?		
3 Have adequate and effective controls been established to measure each task performed by the sales force as shown in Figure 8.2?		

Description of task	Level of performance				Controls used to measure results	Remarks, suggestions, recommendations
1 Achieve sales targets	(a) *New machines*				(a) and (b) Review of sales with manager (on monthly basis) at sales meetings of all significant shortfalls	
		1st Qtr £	2nd Qtr £	3rd Qtr £	4th Qtr £	
	Tractors	62 000	42 000	6 000	48 000	
	Combines	47 000	18 000	18 000	—	
	Balers	8 750	—	9 000	—	
	Ploughs	2 000	2 000	3 000	5 000	
	General machines	6 000	9 000	3 800	3 000	
	Barn machines	6 000	6 000	12 000	1 200	
	Total new machines	131 750	77 000	51 800	57 200	
	(b) *Used*	£	£	£	£	
	Tractors	6 000	30 000	12 000	30 000	
	Combines	—	12 000	18 000	—	
	Others	3 000	2 500	2 500	3 000	
	Total used machines	£9 000	£44 500	£32 500	£33 000	
2 Gain new customers	35 new customers yielding minimum of £42 000 by end of twelve-month period (particular machines may also be specified, e.g. minimum four new baler conquests)				Review prospect cards weekly Review conversion rates monthly Review monthly sales records Identify major prospects and agree customer strategy	
3 Plan to make more profitable use of time	(a) Daily call rate average eight calls at least two prospect calls (b) Daily plan formulated and carried out (c) Average daily mileage 125				Daily submission of report Submission of plans on field visits (a) Journey plans (b) Individual call plans	

Figure 8.2 Example of key analysis for salesmen

Description of task	Level of performance	Controls used to measure results	Remarks, suggestions, recommendations
4 Make sales propositions which are up to the required standard	(a) Sales interview conducted in line with predetermined plan according to general principles of the 'selling cycle' as taught on company courses (b) Product information accurate (c) Arrangements for follow-up clearly agreed with customer	Monthly observation by sales manager	
5 Maximise profitability of sales	(a) Keep to discount limits set by manager (define limits per machine group) (b) Evaluation of used machinery to show on average accuracy of ± 7½ % (c) Achievement of used machinery sales targets	(a) Review of new machinery sales record (b) Review of prices paid for used machinery (c) Review of sales of used machinery	
6 Maintain and make full use of equipment and sales aids	(a) Car in good order and appearance (b) Catalogue up-to-date (c) Literature stock up-to-date and kept in presentable condition (d) Record cards readily available and up-to-date	Observation and inspection by sales manager on field visits	
7 Maintain control over credit and ensure prompt payment of accounts	Keep to agreed predetermined limits (specify limits for each category of client and record on card)	Monthly review of outstanding accounts	

Figure 8.2 Example of key analysis for salesmen —*concluded*

9: The Accompanied Call in Field Sales Management

We have examined five methods of training the field sales manager can use to develop skills on the job. Three of these will be used when accompanying the salesman – demonstration, role playing, and coaching using the ten steps in field sales training technique. The other two, product knowledge by programmed learning and the sales manual, provide a means by which the salesman can carry out a programme of self training.

THE ACCOMPANIED CALL

Prominent among the techniques for managing your sales force and for developing the skills of individual sales personnel is the *accompanied call*.

This is when you, the manager, set aside periods of time to go out with an individual salesman and accompany him as he makes calls on existing and potential customers. By design and necessity you become involved in many different types of accompanied call. And although your ultimate aim may be to observe the selling performance of the salesman and from this detached viewpoint discuss and analyse what has taken place, reality is often very different. The relationship between you and the salesman you are accompanying can be or is seen to be by the customer to range from that of:

- two people both of equal status
- a generalist with a specialist
- a manager with a subordinate.

Whatever the circumstances, the disciplined application of the *Ten Steps in Field Sales Training Techniques* to the accompanied calls will ensure that much more is gained from them by the customer, the salesman and by you the manager. Analysis of accompanied calls reveals five main categories:

1   The public relations call
2   The 'help me' call
3   The dual sell call
4   The demonstration call
5   The observation call

A study of these five categories reveals the temptations and business opportunities they afford.

THE PUBLIC RELATIONS CALL

From time to time your salespeople will earmark certain of their existing or potential customers who, for one reason or another, they would like to be recognised in an appropriate way. This often takes the form of a visit and a lunch hosted by you the manager rather than by the salesman. Whilst such visits are legitimate and necessary, they frequently end up as nothing more than a pleasant chat, a flag waving excuse for your presence by the salesman and an unproductive lunch.

Before such a public relations call, careful questioning and use of steps 1 to 4 of the Ten Step approach (see Figure 8.1) will reveal:

- The commercial opportunities of the visit and the specific sales objective to be achieved in addition to the PR value.
- The on-going development of this customer or prospect and the follow-up action to be taken by the salesman.
- The real value (if any) that the senior manager brings to the customer meeting and the recognition of the much more major part the salesman can and should take in the discussions.
- After this type of call steps 6 to 10 should be carried out to pinpoint opportunities for salesman motivation and development.

THE 'HELP ME' CALL

At the invitation of the salesman, you may be asked to 'help me with this customer problem. It is too big for me to handle'. Which means he wants you to do the selling.

Alternatively, whilst accompanying a salesman, you may say about one of the calls to be made. 'I had better handle this one, but of course you come with me (to drive the car, take notes, or to pick up the pieces if it goes wrong is not said but frequently implied). This is the type of call where it is all too easy to go on an ego trip and show off to your salesman. Remember that the salesman has to live with the implications of your involvement not you. So once again apply the Ten Steps pre and post-call. This will:

- Identify the real problem (if one exists) and why it has gone beyond the perceived ability of the salesman to handle it on his own.
- Identify the training need, be it of knowledge, skill, experience or self-confidence to be tackled to prevent the problem recurring.
- Involve the salesman in finding out what is the best way of tackling this sales interview and how to apply it to this particular customer.
- Make you look for ways in which the salesman can handle the call with you the manager having a planned reserve role rather than the other way round.

THE DUAL SELL CALL

In a dual selling call where both manager and salesman take active roles in the selling, the lessons that should be learned by Steps 6 to 10 after the call are ignored. Indeed if it has gone exceptionally well, largely due to the manager's selling expertise he may look to the salesman for praise e.g. 'I was pretty good don't you agree?' The end result is a frustrated, annoyed demotivated salesman.

In a dual selling call where the manager's specialist knowledge or skill justifies his planned involvement, steps 3 and 4 are of great importance. They discipline you to think about and agree the call plan and classify the role each is to play. From the agreement about these steps prior to the call, manager and salesman can assess them afterwards and the lessons to be learned from success or failure.

THE DEMONSTRATION CALL

The demonstration call properly conducted is the foundation training for all new sales personnel and has a genuine place in the development of the sales force. It is the first of the training opportunities used by a sales manager to establish for the sales trainee the standards of product knowledge, call planning, selling technique and work organisation that he is expected to emulate and hopefully to exceed.

The problems start when a demonstration call is unplanned and originates as a by-product of the 'take over'. A demonstration call must be planned and, using the steps 1 to 4, each part of it explained to the salesman who is to observe it. It is no good expecting a salesman to appreciate the finer points of a manager's demonstration, or to use the call as a learning opportunity when he is smarting from the indignity of having the call snatched away from him and not returned. The salesman's heart and mind are both hostile and it is the manager's fault.

Demonstration calls should be carefully selected and set out to illustrate a specific selling technique or an aspect of product knowledge designed to meet the identified training needs of a new salesman. A structured programme of demonstrator calls is described in Chapter 10 'How to Train New Salesmen'.

The demonstrator must keep religiously to the ten steps for every call he demonstrates. He must explain his own thinking and allow himself to be questioned by the trainee. Earlier in this chapter I mentioned the importance of the manager being a successful salesman so that he can demonstrate competent salesmanship. In imitating what he sees and hears, the trainee must have a greater chance of success than if left to his own devices.

Unless managers are competent in selling, they will either avoid the opportunities that should be taken to demonstrate techniques to new salesmen or avoid detailed discussion of what took place after the demonstration call.

Field sales managers and sales trainers should, like their salespeople, have regular refresher sales training (at least once a year) to maintain their selling competence.

THE OBSERVATION CALL

In practical terms, observation means that on such calls your prime objective as sales manager is to *watch* and to *listen* to the sales interview, and from this detached position you can give the salesman an accurate and helpful analysis of what happened, and what can be learnt from the call and used beneficially in future.

This is the most valuable, and the most difficult of all the accompanied calls. Carried out successfully it enables the field sales manager to evaluate field performance, generate learning, and develop skill and self assessment.

It demands not only the systematic application of the pre and post-call discussion, but the much more difficult skill of being part of the selling call without taking it away from the salesman. 'Observation' does not mean that the manager slides into the room unnoticed by the customer or listens to the conversation behind a screen. Nor does it mean that, once introduced by the salesman, you can sit silent when the customer speaks to you; nor does it mean that when shortcomings of knowledge and skill threaten disaster that you sit impassive, ignoring the anguished pleas for help from the salesman or the questioning glances from the customer.

If drawn into the sales conversation, you must respond courteously and credibly but remember to hand it back to the salesman at the first opportunity. These can be created by the manager with phrases such as:

- 'Yes that is an important point and one that the company has given much thought to, but I know that Peter has some examples of how that problem can become overcome, . . . Peter!'
- 'You are right, discounts are important and Tom's discretion and authority is greater than mine here. He is close to your business and so can negotiate the best overall package for you. Tom, what do you feel is the best way to tackle this?'

Such 'handback' phrases do not just happen. They will come to mind much more easily if the pre-call planning stages of the Ten Steps have been properly and creatively carried out. One of the most frequent causes of management intervention in an accompanied call is the uncertainty of what will follow and a natural inclination to fear the worst if the call is handed back to the salesman.

Provided the salesman and the manager have fully discussed the call plan, the sales objectives, how they are to be achieved and their specific roles, the manager will find it easier to bite his lip or hold his tongue knowing that an opportunity to explain or rectify an omission will come later. Similarly he will be better able to assess the true significance of a 'mistake' made by the salesman in relation to the overall sales objective and will frequently come to realise that patience and disciplined restraint are best.

The accompanied call is an underrated skill. Whatever type of call you are involved in as a manager requires thorough preparation, clarity of purpose in the minds of both you and the salesman and a well developed capability to observe, to analyse and to coach. The Ten Step technique provides a discipline and a proven method for you to develop the selling effectiveness of your salesmen (see Figure 9.1, The accompanied call family tree).

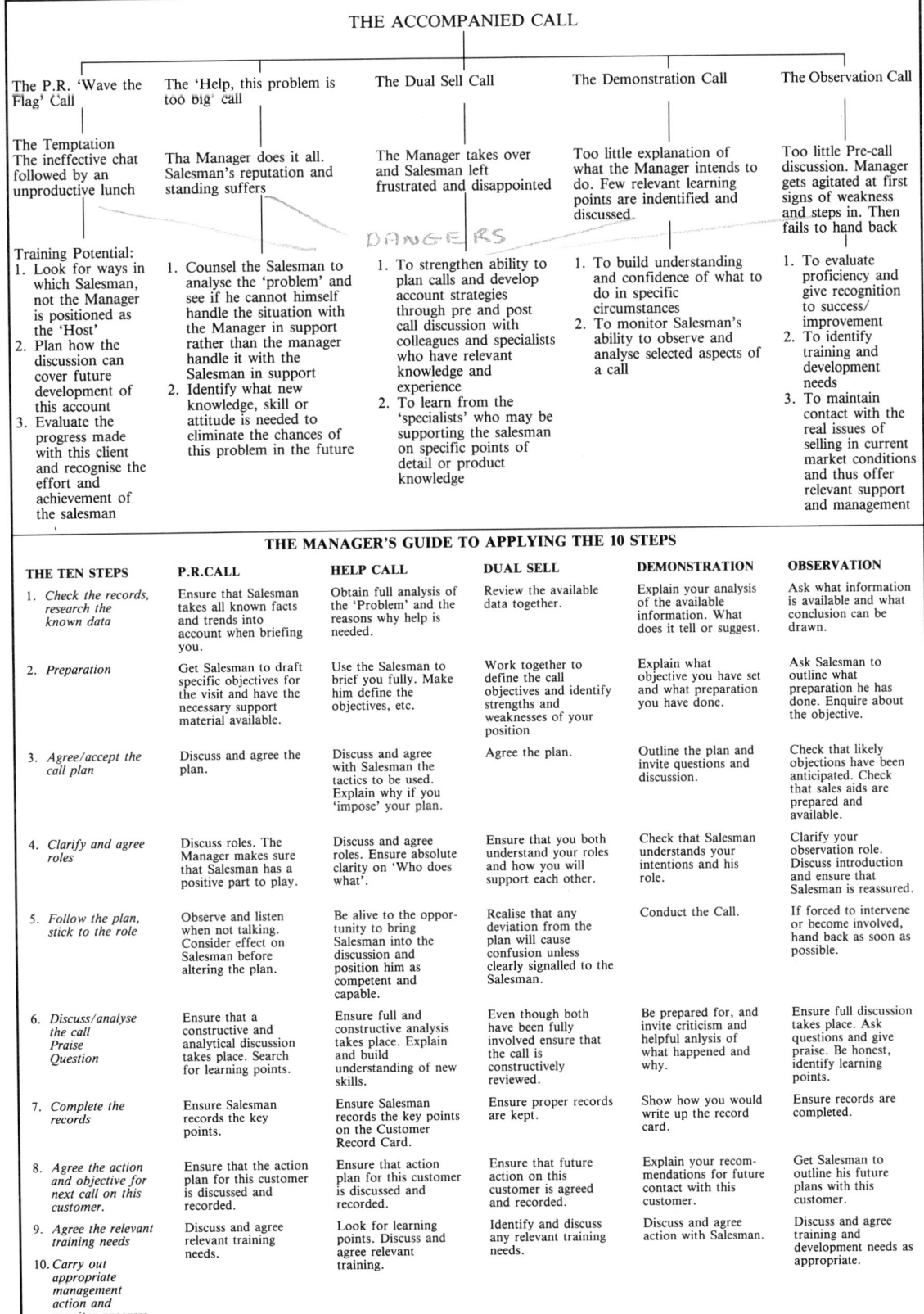

THE ACCOMPANIED CALL

The P.R. 'Wave the Flag' Call	The 'Help, this problem is too big' call	The Dual Sell Call	The Demonstration Call	The Observation Call
The Temptation The ineffective chat followed by an unproductive lunch	Tha Manager does it all. Salesman's reputation and standing suffers	The Manager takes over and Salesman left frustrated and disappointed	Too little explanation of what the Manager intends to do. Few relevant learning points are indentified and discussed	Too little Pre-call discussion. Manager gets agitated at first signs of weakness and steps in. Then fails to hand back

DANGERS

The P.R. 'Wave the Flag' Call	The 'Help, this problem is too big' call	The Dual Sell Call	The Demonstration Call	The Observation Call
Training Potential: 1. Look for ways in which Salesman, not the Manager is positioned as the 'Host' 2. Plan how the discussion can cover future development of this account 3. Evaluate the progress made with this client and recognise the effort and achievement of the salesman	1. Counsel the Salesman to analyse the 'problem' and see if he cannot himself handle the situation with the Manager in support rather than the manager handle it with the Salesman in support 2. Identify what new knowledge, skill or attitude is needed to eliminate the chances of this problem in the future	1. To strengthen ability to plan calls and develop account strategies through pre and post call discussion with colleagues and specialists who have relevant knowledge and experience 2. To learn from the 'specialists' who may be supporting the salesman on specific points of detail or product knowledge	1. To build understanding and confidence of what to do in specific circumstances 2. To monitor Salesman's ability to observe and analyse selected aspects of a call	1. To evaluate proficiency and give recognition to success/improvement 2. To identify training and development needs 3. To maintain contact with the real issues of selling in current market conditions and thus offer relevant support and management

THE MANAGER'S GUIDE TO APPLYING THE 10 STEPS

THE TEN STEPS	P.R.CALL	HELP CALL	DUAL SELL	DEMONSTRATION	OBSERVATION
1. *Check the records, research the known data*	Ensure that Salesman takes all known facts and trends into account when briefing you.	Obtain full analysis of the 'Problem' and the reasons why help is needed.	Review the available data together.	Explain your analysis of the available information. What does it tell or suggest.	Ask what information is available and what conclusion can be drawn.
2. *Preparation*	Get Salesman to draft specific objectives for the visit and have the necessary support material available.	Use the Salesman to brief you fully. Make him define the objectives, etc.	Work together to define the call objectives and identify strengths and weaknesses of your position	Explain what objective you have set and what preparation you have done.	Ask Salesman to outline what preparation he has done. Enquire about the objective.
3. *Agree/accept the call plan*	Discuss and agree the plan.	Discuss and agree with Salesman the tactics to be used. Explain why if you 'impose' your plan.	Agree the plan.	Outline the plan and invite questions and discussion.	Check that likely objections have been anticipated. Check that sales aids are prepared and available.
4. *Clarify and agree roles*	Discuss roles. The Manager makes sure that Salesman has a positive part to play.	Discuss and agree roles. Ensure absolute clarity on 'Who does what'.	Ensure that you both understand your roles and how you will support each other.	Check that Salesman understands your intentions and his role.	Clarify your observation role. Discuss introduction and ensure that Salesman is reassured.
5. *Follow the plan, stick to the role*	Observe and listen when not talking. Consider effect on Salesman before altering the plan.	Be alive to the opportunity to bring Salesman into the discussion and position him as competent and capable.	Realise that any deviation from the plan will cause confusion unless clearly signalled to the Salesman.	Conduct the Call.	If forced to intervene or become involved, hand back as soon as possible.
6. *Discuss/analyse the call* *Praise* *Question*	Ensure that a constructive and analytical discussion takes place. Search for learning points.	Ensure full and constructive analysis takes place. Explain and build understanding of new skills.	Even though both have been fully involved ensure that the call is constructively reviewed.	Be prepared for, and invite criticism and helpful anlysis of what happened and why.	Ensure full discussion takes place. Ask questions and give praise. Be honest, identify learning points.
7. *Complete the records*	Ensure Salesman records the key points.	Ensure Salesman records the key points on the Customer Record Card.	Ensure proper records are kept.	Show how you would write up the record card.	Ensure records are completed.
8. *Agree the action and objective for next call on this customer.*	Ensure that the action plan for this customer is discussed and recorded.	Ensure that action plan for this customer is discussed and recorded.	Ensure that future action on this customer is agreed and recorded.	Explain your recommendations for future contact with this customer.	Get Salesman to outline his future plans with this customer.
9. *Agree the relevant training needs*	Discuss and agree relevant training needs.	Look for learning points. Discuss and agree relevant training.	Identify and discuss any relevant training needs.	Discuss and agree action with Salesman.	Discuss and agree training and development needs as appropriate.
10. *Carry out appropriate management action and monitor progress*					

Figure 9.1 The accompanied call family tree

10:

How to Train New Salesmen

The initial on-the-job sales training given to new people on joining a company has a powerful influence on their subsequent attitude to selling, their motivation to sell and the results they produce from their selling. Good habits can be picked up just as easily as bad ones. Indeed, in selling, good habits have a cumulative effect because they produce sales results faster than bad ones.

WHAT IS A NEW SALESMAN?

A new salesman – for the purpose of initial training in selling technique – is any one of the following: a person on his first day with a new company; a person taking over his sales territory after joining the company; a person joining his field sales manager after completing the company's induction training course; a person, transferred from another department of a company, joining the sales force and taking over a sales territory.

No matter what the circumstances are, all these categories of new salesman need training at the outset of their selling career. This goes, too, for people who come from another company where they were employed as salesmen and may well have had training there. They still need to be introduced to the 'way we do things here', or how the selling is done. Obviously, the field sales manager will gauge the amount of knowledge and skill such a person needs, and how basic the approach should be, and does not insult the self-perception of competence that he might have.

OBJECTIVES TO BE ACHIEVED

By the completion of the period set aside for the on-the-job initial training of a new salesman, the field sales manager should have achieved three objectives:

1   *Established good working habits.* The field sales manager will want to establish that the new salesman develops good working habits in planning his sales work as a whole, planning each sales interview in advance, and ensuring from the outset a high standard of quality, accuracy and regularity in dealing with paper work and sales administration. He will especially want to instil the habit of recording and analysing key customer information on the customer cards so that every sales interview is based upon individual customer needs.

2   *Established his selling technique on a firm basis.* If the salesman comes into the field having already been given basic classroom training or an induction course this is very helpful. In such circumstances the manager's job will be that much easier. In many companies, including one of the most successful international food manufacturers, the salesman joins his field sales manager on the first day in the company. This places an enormous responsibility on his manager to ensure that the sales training is imparted speedily and effectively.

3   *Motivate and build self-confidence.* Most successful people can point to some one or a particular manager who put them on the first rung of the ladder to success. The first rung of the ladder for a salesman is made by the first training he receives, and by the knowledge and proof that it opens, rather than closes, the door to the sales results he needs to satisfy his manager, the company and himself. No one can better build such self-confidence than his manager.

HOW LONG SHOULD INITIAL ON-THE-JOB TRAINING LAST?

Opinions and policies vary from company to company about how much time a field sales manager sets aside for the initial field training of new salesmen. With few notable exceptions, insufficient time is devoted to it. It is a sad reflection on the attitude of companies to their market places that it is the major food groups and fast-moving consumer goods companies (where competition is greatest) who invest the most time in training their new salesmen. It is perhaps also not too surprising that these companies are the most profitable. Many of their erstwhile salesmen today are the managing directors, marketing directors and sales directors of banking, port services, capital goods, and consumer durable companies.

Since no two salesmen learn at the same speed, the field sales manager must allow sufficient time to achieve his training objectives with the new salesmen. At least two weeks should be allocated to this training.

METHOD OF TRAINING THE NEW SALESMAN

How the manager will allocate the time he sets aside to train a new salesman will be governed by the individual's capacity to learn, by his power to assimilate, and by his ability to translate new knowledge and techniques into practice. The plan will be based on a period of two weeks' training (see Figure 10.1).

Week one

The make-up of the first week would be broadly on the following lines. The manager should spend the whole of the first working week in the field accompanying the new salesman. The first two days will be devoted to ensuring that the new man is taught the principles of selling and how they relate to the products or services he will sell. If he has already attended a company induction course at which selling techniques were taught, then the manager's aim will be to ensure that the man can fit what he learnt on this course into the framework of the selling job as it is performed in the field.

Week One	Objectives	Methods
Monday	To establish good work habits in planning, organisation and control of sales administration	Manager goes through the planning and reporting systems for sales activity: how and why calls should be planned in advance; the value to the salesman, the customer and the company, of completed customer record cards; how each sales call should be planned. The salesman is asked to apply knowledge taught by planning his first week's work with the help of the manager
Tuesday	To establish selling technique on a firm basis	Manager plans a number of calls showing the salesman why he is calling, what he intends to do in each call and how he will do it. The salesman is asked to observe a particular aspect of each call as in Figure 10.2
Wednesday	To develop the salesman's selling skills	Salesman takes some not too difficult calls, preparing each one with the help of the manager. Where necessary opening or closing techniques will be rehearsed
Thursday	To motivate and build the salesman's self-confidence and belief that he can sell	Salesman takes all selling calls, the manager observing how he prepares, how he conducts each call and what happens. After each call a 'kerbside conference' is conducted
Friday	To review the week's work and plan the work to be done in the second week demonstrating the importance of forward planning to achieve planned results	Morning spent by salesman continuing to handle calls. After lunch salesman and manager review the week's work in terms of what has happened and what has been achieved. Manager then helps salesman to plan and prepare second week's work
Week Two	Objectives	Methods
Monday	To continue development of selling skills and building self-confidence of salesman	Manager joins salesman at start of day. Checks the man's understanding of week's and day's programme, and then uses the ten steps technique to help the salesman prepare call and to coach him after each one is completed. At the end of the day manager reviews calls, tells man what progress has been made and where he needs to strengthen his technique, then leaves salesman
Tuesday Wednesday Thursday	To allow the salesman to demonstrate his selling skill by handling all selling calls unobserved and unaccompanied	Salesman spends three days on his own carrying out his selling calls and recording how he planned and conducted them and what happened
Friday	To appraise progress and identify future training needs of salesman	Manager rejoins salesman. Before first calls are made, reviews the past three days and what successes salesman achieved and congratulate if possible on them. Salesman carries out calls planned for day, manager using 'ten steps' for one or two specially selected and important ones
		At end of day manager and salesman carry out first salesman performance appraisal and decide further training needs and how they will be satisfied
		Manager summarises day, man's progress and encourages him. Agrees date for next field visit and date for submitting first salesman self-appraisal

Figure 10.1 Initial on-the-job training of the new salesman

Initially, as his trainer, the manager should conduct the first selling calls made to demonstrate how selling techniques are applied and to establish the standard of salesmanship the new salesman must reach and exceed.

On every selling call where the manager does the selling with the new man observing, the salesman will only benefit if before each call the manager carries out the first two steps in training: prepare and tell – tell him what is going to be achieved in the call and how. To prepare and plan a demonstration call, use a call-plan format (see Figure 4.1) which can be referred back to after the call has been made. The manager should prepare his demonstration calls with the new salesman, telling him the following steps in his call plan:

1 Why the call is being made: its specific objective.
2 What it is hoped will be achieved: quantify the objective, e.g. the order size or commitment.
3 What opening will be used: what questions will be used to explore and identify the customer's needs or problems.
4 What benefits will be presented: in what order and how will they be related to satisfying anticipated customer's needs.
5 What objections are anticipated: how they will be handled.
6 What closing techniques will be used: how the pre-set call objective decided will be achieved.
7 How the manager and new salesman will introduce themselves to customer.
8 What part the new salesman will take in the call.
9 What particular features of the sales interview the new salesman should observe.

This briefing should be carried out before every call and for every call made by the manager in his role as a salesman demonstrating sales technique.

The sales interview is a very dynamic and often fast moving situation. It is quite difficult for a new man to follow all the stages through which it passes and how the selling techniques change and influence the sale. For this reason the manager's demonstration calls should be planned so

Calls made by manager	Training objective
First call	To observe a selling call carried out in its entirety
Second call	To observe how the interview is opened, the way questions get the buyer talking about his needs
Third call	To observe how benefits are presented and related to the buyer's identified needs, how visual aids are used and when; how third party references are made; how the acceptance or otherwise of benefits is assessed by check questions
Fourth call	To observe which objections arise and if anticipated how dealt with; if not anticipated how handled; how objections can help the sale
Fifth call	To observe what close is made to achieve the call objective and how it is attempted and how initiative is kept if commitment is refused or not given
Sixth call	To observe how a selling call is carried out in its entirety and how the component parts fit together into a persuasive planned conversation directed by the manager towards a planned sales objective

Figure 10.2 Observation of selling techniques in practice

that as far as it is humanly possible to contrive it, the salesman concentrates his attention on observing how a specific sales technique is used. The salesman will learn how to use these techniques much better if he observes them in sequence as people learn how to satisfy their needs (see Figure 10.2).

During the third day the manager should be able to give some of the less difficult selling calls to the new salesman. The preparation for these calls must be thorough and the manager should role play important parts, such as the opening and close, or dealing with objections. The manager on these occasions should play the part of the customer realistically. The value of these preparatory role playing sessions will be greatly increased if the manager has a portable tape recorder to playback the session and let the salesman hear what he actually sounds like as he employs the techniques he has been taught and so far only observed.

This is the third step in the method of training: having the salesman actually perform. It is therefore essential that again for each of these vital first selling calls the man handles, a call plan is used. After each call the manager should carry out a 'kerbside conference' (see Figure 10.3).

On the last two working days of the first week, the new salesman should handle most, if not all, the selling calls. There is always a danger during the first week, of the manager grasping the opportunity to escape back into selling and take most of the calls himself. *People learn more by doing than by watching.* It is therefore more productive to the development of his skills for the new salesman to do two or three calls under the manager's guidance at this stage than to watch him do all the calls for a day.

In the late afternoon of the last working day of this week the manager and the new salesman should set aside at least two hours to plan the second week's work. The plan should cover the whole week and include:

1   Deciding the numbers and types of customers to be seen and the sales targets to set to achieve the volume/units required for the week.
2   Identifying the decision makers to be seen at each call.
3   Using the telephone to make as many firm appointments as possible.
4   Checking with head office to obtain current information about any of the customers to be seen which might influence the outcome of each call, e.g. accounts paid, accounts overdue, letters of complaint about late delivery, orders received, bankruptcies, change of ownership, etc.

Neither the manager's car nor his home are the ideal places to do this planning. If possible use a hotel lounge where there is quiet and freedom from any distractions.

Finally, before parting company at the end of the first week the manager should remember that it has been a fairly traumatic one for the salesman. Congratulate him on what he has done well, encourage him by the prospect of next week solving some of the difficulties he has encountered, and send him home in a *positive* frame of mind feeling that he has achieved something worthwhile.

Week two

The field sales manager will have decided at the end of the first week if the new salesman has made good progress, or whether it has been very slow and he will need to spend a lot more time in field accompaniment.

Provided the man made a good start in the first week his manager should aim to spend the *first* and *last* working days of the second week with him on his sales territory. The purpose of these two days will be to ensure that on the first day of the second working week the new man starts with a disciplined and planned approach to his selling job, helped by the presence and

The discussion	Notes
Manager: Well, how do you think it went?	*Immediate involvement by questioning*
Salesman: Pretty well. I got the order, didn't I?	
M Yes, well done. That's the major objective, of course. But do you think it was the right order	*Sincere praise. Manager beginning to probe*
S Well, I don't think he could have taken any more stock of the product. He doesn't have the space	
M What about our other products?	*Manager exposing limitations of call objective*
S I suppose I could have introduced one or two of the new quality lines. But the opportunity didn't arise	
M Is there anything that could have been done to create an opening?	*Showing that the call could have been better prepared*
S Quite honestly I was so pleased with the order that I forgot about anything else	*Salesman admits that once he got the order he did not continue (very common mistake)*
M Perhaps if you had planned the call better, might you have built in a mention?	*Manager still questioning – identified call planning weakness*
S I suppose so. But in any case as you heard, the buyer says he has no space for any more products	
M Yes, what about that objection? Did you believe he meant that?	*Manager now probing second weakness*
S His shelves certainly looked full	*Salesman beginning to get defensive*
M But won't he have to stock somebody's quality line. Our research as you know shows that the market is trending that way: 20% of the customers are now in this segment, aren't they?	*Manager identifying possible objection answer*
S Yes, I should have mentioned it. I guess what he really meant was that he's happy with his current supplier of that type of product	*Salesman shifting ground*
M Would you not have uncovered his real reason if you had pressed a little harder there?	
S I've never been good at that kind of thing. It can only lead to an argument	*Salesman very defensive. This is the third different attempt to justify his failure to press the buyer*
M Not necessarily. Anyway we can come back to that later. Overall how would you summarise that interview?	*Manager at fault. Should have gently pursued until gained acceptance. He will now have to tell the salesman of the deficiency*

Figure 10.3 A typical 'kerbside conference'

The discussion	Notes
S	Well, on the good side, I got an order but I suppose with a bit better planning I could have got some of the new products in. But I don't know how if the man simply didn't have the space	*More balanced view than originally from salesman. Recognises his planning failure but still defensive over the space objection*
M	Well. let's take those two points of preparation and objection handling. First the basic aim of preparation is to ensure we have specific objectives for each call. This avoids the danger that the call might simply be a rambling conversation. From these defined targets which are derived from a study of the customer record card we can structure the whole interview – how to open, what to present in what order, what objections are likely and how to close. You probably remember we spent a lot of time on this on the initial training programme?	*Manager now instructs* *Links instruction back to initial training*
S	Yes, now you remind me—it's called structuring, isn't it?	*Salesman beginning to remember*
M	That's right. It makes sure we don't overlook opportunities simply because we've got an order for something. It also helps particularly in predicting objections. Knowing this buyer and knowing you wished to introduce new lines, could you not have forecast that he would object that he had no space?	*Back to the space objection. Manager still having to try and gain acceptance*
S	Yes, I suppose so. He's always moaning that he hasn't got enough room. And he gets upset if you push him	*Salesman still defensive*
M	Quite understandably. You must agree with him that his space is limited but you could have brought the research with you and shown him how the market is changing. Perhaps he would have realised then that he cannot afford to overlook this important group of customers. Also as the research was done by an independent agency, it is not you that he has to argue with. Remember – we called this the Third Party Reference or Testimonial technique?	*Manager instructing now. His points are perfectly valid but could lose impact because of failure to really identify nature of salesman's lack of skill*
S	That's right. But I didn't have the survey with me. I don't really understand this research business, you know. The boys and I have often said it baffles us	*At last, the salesman admits he does not really understand the research*
M	Right, we will discuss the use of research surveys at the next sales meeting. But before that meeting, which is a week on Tuesday, I want you to read the latest survey and make sure you always have it with you. It contains many good sales points. Also I want you to re-read the training notes on preparation and objection handling techniques. In fact, it would be valuable if you could give a session at the meeting after next on 'How I plan my calls'. Pop in next time you are in the office and we will discuss it in more detail. Now for the next call, let's start practising some preparation. Get out your record card and let's see if we can't get some specific goals. You did very well to get an order at all. You can do better next time and get a bigger one.	*Manager specifies action and time periods. Note linking of field training to sales meetings as research problem probably common in sales force. Manager should also note for possible inclusion in initial training. Self-training specified and linked to action.* *Delegation but with accountability. Training continues on call preparation. Probably to be followed by rehearsal and role-playing of handling space objection.* *Final words of encouragement.*

Figure 10.3 A typical 'kerbside conference' —*concluded*

reassurance of his manager, and to introduce the ten steps technique as a discipline field sales training. It will also allow the manager to review on the last working day the new man's work and to carry out the first performance appraisal.

First day
On the first day the manager should spend the major part of his time implementing the ten steps technique; he should avoid taking any selling calls himself unless there has been a marked deterioration in some aspect of technique which he feels should be demonstrated.

At the completion of work on this day the manager should tell the man where he has made headway, the areas needing strengthening and what to do about them.

The salesman will work on his own on Tuesday, Wednesday and Thursday, the manager rejoins him first thing on Friday for the final accompaniment of his initial training period.

Last day
Before starting the day's selling calls, the manager should briefly discuss the calls the salesman has made and successes he has had since Monday; congratulate him on any successes achieved but leave detailed analysis of failures until the end of the day. Then after checking the programme for the day, get on with it. The manager will be able to observe the quantity and quality of selling performance following a period of three days when the man has been working on his own.

At the completion of the day's calls, manager and salesman should retire to a quiet hotel lounge to carry out a most important activity: the salesman's first performance appraisal. This will take time. It is not something to rush through because the decisions the appraisal will help to make will influence the motivation of the salesman and the training his manager maps out for the immediate future.

Each section of the form should be discussed in the light of the calls made, what happened, and the results achieved. Before expressing any opinion or making an assessment, the salesman should be asked how he would rate himself for each factor. This will tell the field sales manager how self-perceptive he is. The manager can then give his views and his rating for each factor.

The completed appraisal provides both the salesman and the manager with an initial assessment of the training completed so far, the results it has produced, and the areas identified where further help will be needed. A copy of the manager's first appraisal should be given to the salesman.

Before parting company the manager should agree two actions with the salesman. First, he should arrange the date for his next field training visit. Second, the salesman should complete a salesman performance appraisal, indicating his personal appraisal of his own selling performance, on a given date just before the next field training visit, and send a copy of this form to his manager. This self-appraisal will provide a useful basis for discussing progress and areas of training need.

Action planning checklist

	Answers	Action and timing
1 Does the company have an initial field training programme for new salesmen joining the company such as shown in Figure 10.1?		
2 Have the field sales management been trained to train new salesmen in the field? If not, what steps will be taken to train them?		
3 Is the period set aside for the initial field training of new salesmen sufficient?		
4 Is the salesman performance-appraisal system introduced to the new salesmen during their initial field training?		
5 Is there an effective method of follow-up field training for the new salesmen?		
6 If new salesmen are intially sent out for training with experienced salesmen, have these experienced salesmen been trained in field sales training?		

11:

How to Train Experienced Salesmen

The individual training and development of every salesman begins when he joins a company and only ends when he leaves it. It does not stop with the raw recruit. Field training of experienced salesmen, including the best in the team, should be tackled not only with the same thoroughness as for new salesmen but also on a *planned, regular basis*.

The development of experienced salesmen is perhaps one of the greatest flaws in the overall sales training policy of the majority of companies, both large and small. Why is this? There seem to be three reasons. First, few companies have recognised that the training of experienced salesmen differs from that given to newly recruited salesmen. Second, the benefits of training experienced salesmen in terms of even better sales results, a fresh approach to old sales problems, and greater job satisfaction, are insufficiently recognised. Third, and this is perhaps the main reason, many field sales managers are apprehensive about going out and training some of their most experienced salesmen. They do not recognise that the observer need not be as skilled as the participant in order to train well.

WHAT IS AN EXPERIENCED SALESMAN?

Whilst it is easy to define a new salesman, whom do we classify as an experienced salesman for the purposes of training and development? Opinions will differ between the sales managers of speciality products, consumer goods and services, and those managing industrial sales forces. But under the broad heading of experienced salesmen we can identify two main categories and these will represent the bulk of the salesmen with whom most field sales managers will invest their time.

The first category is the salesman entering his second year of service with a company. He has survived the doubts and fears of whether he can do the job. For the field sales manager this salesman presents the biggest challenge to his skill as a trainer. In this year the salesman can either become a finely tuned polished professional or a cynical and disillusioned one who starts looking at the jobs column in the *Daily Telegraph*.

The second category are those salesmen who have been with a company three years and more. These people invariably stay with the company and many will become career salesmen. Sadly they tend to be neglected by the field sales manager. They tend to become satisfied with their own performances and with average results, to be complacent about the level of sales they are producing yet at the same time resistant to sales training. Yet in terms of salaries and related overheads these are the most expensive members of the sales force. The field sales manager should therefore invest time in them so that he obtains the optimum yield for the capital invested. (Presumably he would not invest £1000 of his own money in shares in a company and be happy to see the yield diminish year by year and take no action!)

WHAT OBJECTIVES ARE TO BE ACHIEVED?

Only by accompanying his salesmen as frequently as possible and on a planned basis can the field sales manager accurately and effectively: *identify* individual standards of sales performance, strengths and weaknesses; *measure* these performances against the standards set; ascertain the *real* reasons for any gap between the two *and agree them with the salesman*; carry out training and coaching; and ensure that as a result these standards are met, maintained, and continuously improved.

To achieve all these aims with experienced salesmen calls for a high degree of skill by the field sales manager. This skill must be used with a sensitivity designed to create an atmosphere of trust and confidence between the salesman and his manager. This will ensure that his salesmen: *welcome* the managers's presence and *agree* standards of performance; *accept* his training assistance in reaching the standards they have agreed; learn *willingly* and *quickly* from the skilled training given; and put the skills into effect *after* the training has been given.

On every field training visit, the objectives of the field sales manager should be:

1 To measure the salesman's performance against the standards which have been set and agreed.
2 To find out what his specific strengths and weaknesses are.
3 To agree these with him.
4 To correct weaknesses and improve on strengths by training.
5 To encourage and coach and show how selling techniques can be improved.
6 To measure the improvements which result from training.

ANALYSIS OF SALES PERFORMANCE

Before any plans can be made to accompany a particular salesman, the field sales manager must first measure and analyse each person's performance against the standards which have been set and agreed, e.g. sales volume or units sold; new business developed with existing customers; new accounts opened; cost per call; number of effective calls made; ratio of orders to calls; outstanding debtors; number of promotions agreed.

Compare what the salesman has achieved against the standards set for each of these tasks with the salesman's last field appraisal form. These two pieces of information tell the manager the quantity of work done by the salesman and indicate the quality of the selling that went into producing these results.

Note carefully the areas where there has been a marked as well as a sustained improvement. Then identify the most notable and persistent weaknesses in performance. During this analysis, the action taken so far to correct shortcomings in sales technique, work organisation or product knowledge, should be reviewed. Similarly, the reports of field visits by other sales executives, such as the sales training officer, should be considered.

Having completed such a periodic analysis of sales performances, the field sales manager can now prepare the individual training of his salesmen.

PREPARING INDIVIDUAL TRAINING

One of the basic errors made by many newly appointed field sales managers (and some experienced ones too) is to try and cover too much ground when on a training visit to a salesman. This is due in part to a faulty analysis of what is wrong with a man's technique. The fact that he shows an increasing tendency not to close each sale may be due to a failure to set specific sales objectives for each call, rather than any shortcomings in his closing technique. But more often managers overestimate their powers of communication and underestimate the limited amount of knowledge which can be absorbed at any one time. It is better and more effective to improve one technique than to try and attempt three or four.

There are three elements in preparing individual training:

1 *Setting the training objective.* The field sales manager must base the field training of his staff upon a specific objective set in measurable terms so that improvements can be clearly seen by him and the salesman, e.g. to increase the number of general practitioner calls from five to six per day by better work organisation by . . . . . . (a specified date); to ensure that point of sale material is placed in all key accounts by improving merchandising skills by . . . . . . (a specified date); to increase the number of fork lift truck demonstrations from seven to nine per week by improving prospecting techniques by . . . . . . (a specified date).

2 *Planning how this training objective will be achieved.* Field sales training techniques can take many forms, of which the 'kerbside conference' is probably the best known. The field sales manager needs to decide which form of training will be most appropriate and effective to develop the man he is planning to accompany, e.g. role-playing real situations in a hotel room, practice in the car using a portable tape recorder, the manager planning a particular call with the salesman and demonstrating how he uses a particular technique, or coaching using the ten steps technique. Plan the length of time to be spent with the salesman and decide what the respective roles of the manager and the salesman will be. Plan what is going to be said to the salesman about his performance and, above all, how it will be said.

3 *Preparing the salesman.* When the field sales manager has planned to spend one or a number of days with a salesman, he should warn the salesman in sufficient time. There is neither virtue nor value in taking a salesman unawares. Training and policing salesmen should be totally divorced from one another. Some managers just telephone the salesman the night before they are going to accompany him. This is insufficient warning. It is better to write to him so that he knows what the purpose of the field sales manager's visit is and what will happen, e.g.

To: J. Brown   Territory 7
From: W. Smith   Area Manager
Dear Joe
When we were last out together on 15 July we agreed that during my next visit we would concentrate on the three types of benefits you need to emphasise more skilfully when selling our butterfly valves to specifiers. So that we can continue to develop this important area I plan to spend three days with you from 29 to 31 August inclusive.
Looking forward to spending three productive days together.
Yours sincerely,
Bill Smith

HOW LONG TO DEVOTE TO TRAINING EACH SALESMAN

When the Institute of Advanced Motorists designed their test for motorists, they made it long enough to ensure that any fundamental mistakes in driving skill would be revealed. Most of us can drive a car without breaking any of the cardinal rules of the road for about thirty minutes, but to do so for two to three hours calls for a much higher standard of sustained driving skill. The field sales manager should apply the same principles to the field sales training of individual salesmen. But very few do.

Linked to the length of time that should be devoted to training each salesman in the team, is the frequency of such visits. In Chapter 2, I mentioned the fact that the majority of salesmen are unsupervised for over ninety percent of their working lives. And paradoxically the more experienced a man or woman is the less frequently they are visited, yet the company's financial investment in such people is considerable. The *total* annual cost of employing a salesman is very high. It usually exceeds the salary paid to the company's chief executive. When a field sales manager is asked; 'how often in a period of thirty days would you check your capital if you had such a sum of money invested in stocks and shares?' the invariable answer given is 'every day'. Selling is a social skill and, like friendship it is in constant need of repair. As a general rule the more refusals a salesman receives from potential customers the greater should be the frequency of field visits to him by his first line field sales manager. Those who sell speciality products such as double glazing, home improvements, financial incentive schemes, life assurance, encyclopaedias, the category 6 and 7 types of sales job in particular are the most likely to face rejections of their sales propositions several times a day. Consequently they need frequent firm supportive field management.

A survey of the frequency of field training visits with experienced salesmen was carried out in 1971 for the Institute of Marketing of the frequency of field training visits in 3060 companies. It included companies in repeat consumer, intermediate, consumer durable, repeat industrial, capital equipment and services product categories. This showed that, across all these categories, 86 per cent of companies' salesmen had training visits by their sales managers of once a month or less and 67 per cent had training visits only once every two months or less.

I carried out a random check of 100 field sales managers from each of these product category companies. They were asked 'How long do you spend with an individual salesman on any one on-the-job field training visit?' The answers were as follows:

Length of training visit	No. of Field Sales Managers
Half a day (09.00 hrs. to 12.30)	63
One whole day (09.00 hrs. to 17.00)	31
Two whole days	4
Three whole days	2
	100

FREQUENCY OF FIELD TRAINING VISITS TO SALESMEN ACROSS DIFFERENT MARKETS

During the last twelve months, I have collected figures which show that for the majority of salesmen the bulk of their selling time is *unobserved* and *unsupervised*. Yet the markets in which they sell have become much more competitive, the selling job harder and the frequency of customer refusals has increased dramatically as more companies compete with each other for

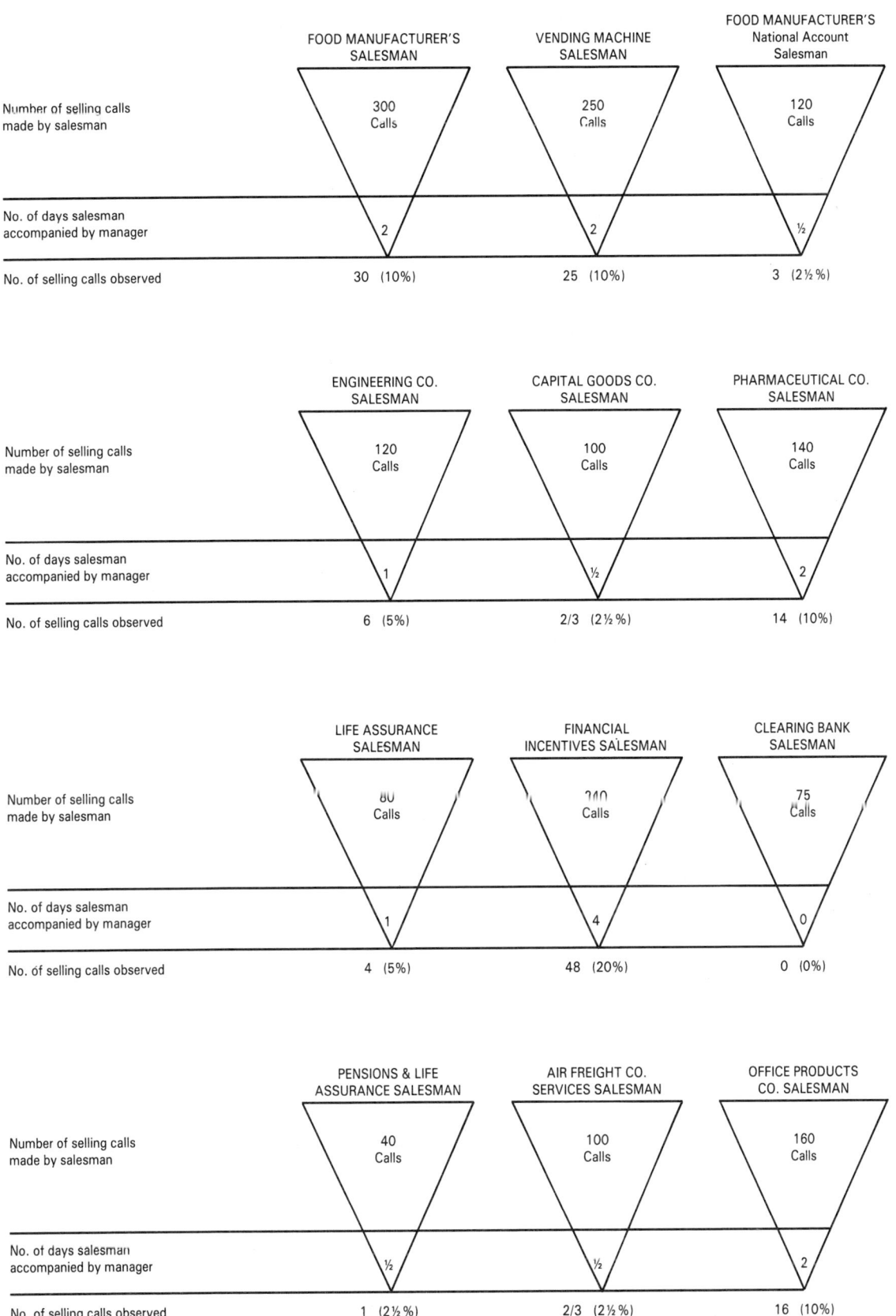

Figure 11.1 Frequency of field visits by field sales managers in different markets in any 20 working days

orders and sales. You may be surprised to learn that in the USA the frequency of field training visits by field sales managers is lower than in Europe and the United Kingdom. The examples in Figure 11.1 show the total number of selling calls made by salesmen in their respective markets in an average working month of 20 days. These selling calls are made up of calls on existing customers, servicing calls and pioneering calls prospecting for new business. In each example is shown the average number of days when an individual salesman is accompanied by his sales or field sales manager responsible for his training and development. These figures indicate the number of actual selling calls *observed* by the manager in relation to the total number of calls made.

Half a day spent with a salesman is insufficient to assess either the effect of your previous training or how he is currently performing, especially if he has 'fixed' some calls to deliberately give you a false impression or if at every call he makes he is unable to see the decision maker.

The minimum amount of time a field sales manager should spend on any one training visit to a salesman will depend upon three factors:

1   The number of calls he needs to observe the salesman handle to assess his current selling skill.
2   The length of time needed to correct any shortcomings in technique.
3   The number of calls the manager needs to observe following coaching to measure whether the shortcoming has been corrected and the improved performance is being maintained.

The evidence in the last two years from pharmaceutical companies, some food manufacturers, and a number of industrial organisations shows that more field sales managers are moving towards allocating at least two days for each field training visit to a salesman. In one very successful service company employing over 500 pioneering, servicing and key-account salesmen, the field sales managers spend three days with each salesman planned as follows:

Day one

Spend the whole day observing the salesman's performance and then compare it with the findings and training contained in the previous field accompaniment. At the end of the day's calls, review the man's performance with him, agree specific improvements to be aimed at, and decide how training will be carried out on the second day.

Day two

Coach the salesman; handle each call as a training exercise using the ten steps in field sales training.

Day three

Observe the day's selling calls handled by the salesman and note on the appraisal form what improvements have been achieved.

Such an investment of time is desirable where a salesman only makes, say, five or six calls per day. Similarly, where a man sells specialities such as consumer durables, insurance, etc. and faces constant rejection, the need for sustained training and development to repair eroded selling technique and morale is considerable.

On the following pages are described a method of training experienced salesmen based on the field sales manager spending two days with him. The same principles suitably adjusted can be used for one day. This is illustrated in Figure 11.2.

HOW SHOULD TRAINING BE CARRIED OUT?

When the field sales manager sets out to meet the salesman for a one, two or three-day period of training, the first objective must always be to create a satisfactory atmosphere in which real training can take place. The manager should aim to arrive first at the designated meeting place, thus setting a good example. He should then make sure that there are no problems worrying the salesman which may colour or prejudice his attitude to the training, such as any domestic difficulties at home, an irate customer, or a pompous memo sent thoughtlessly from someone in the accounts department.

Mention any particular achievement by the salesman, such as a new account opened, or a letter of thanks received from one of his customers.

Next remind him of the object of the visit, what it is hoped will be achieved, and what the role of the field sales manager will be in the calls that are to be made jointly.

Day's Timetable	Objectives	Methods
08.15	Manager joins the salesman for an agreed one-day field training visit to create a positive atmosphere in which to develop the salesman's selling skills	Manager congratulates the salesman on any outstanding achievements since last seen; checks the day's programme of calls, any interesting situations, and how the salesman plans to achieve his day's objectives. Agrees how manager will be introduced at each call
09.00 to 12.30 hrs	To observe how planned sales calls are carried out and what results are achieved To compare present strengths and weaknesses with those identified on last visit	Manager asks salesman before each call to tell him why he is calling, who he is seeing and how he will conduct the call; observes each call; after each call, notes his assessment of what happened on a Call Evaluation Form. Reserves his comments on any critical aspects revealed
12.30 to 13.45 hrs	To analyse selling performance with salesman Identify and agree area(s) needing strengthening To agree action to be taken to achieve agreed objectives	Manager congratulates salesman on his successes; discusses the calls in turn, asking the salesman to assess what happened; agrees any problems which arose and the skill or shortcomings that created them; agrees training to correct them and how
13.45 to 17.30 hrs	To improve selling performance by developing skill in area(s) identified as a problem	Manager uses afternoon's calls as basis for carrying out agreed training, eg role playing before each call, using 'ten steps', etc.
17.30 hrs	To identify improvements achieved through training and areas for further self-training and development	Manager and salesman appraise the day's work and agree strengths improved and steps still to be taken for development; date for next self-appraisal to be submitted and for next field training visit by manager arranged

Figure 11.2 One-day field training visit programme

Day one: Morning

Training objective: To observe how sales calls are handled
Before starting the calls, ask the salesman to outline his plans for the rest of the day. Ask him what sales target he hopes to achieve and what calls will be made. Discuss any particularly interesting sales situations and how he plans to achieve his objectives.

Before each call, ask the salesman to analyse the customer record card and to tell you what he aims to achieve. Ask him how he plans to go about it and agree that you will take no part in the call.

During the call, observe what happens, looking for: changes from the plan outlined, why they occurred, and their effect on the outcome of the call; whether the call objective was achieved.

After the call, the field sales manager should confine his comments to: recognition of the man's successes and strengths in the call; the commercial situation in the call; and clarification of anything that happened where it is necessary to ask the salesman to describe his thinking.

Avoid the temptation, whilst observing, to pass any judgements.

Record observations by making notes and rating what happened in each call using the call evaluation form shown in Figure 11.3. Alternatively, for a large number of observed selling calls, use the form shown in Figure 5.2 on page 38.

It is particularly important to record verbatim key comments made by the salesman and by the customer in a call. These help to bring back the situation much more clearly when each call and what happened is reviewed.

Day one: Lunchtime

Training objective: To analyse salesman's selling performance in calls
Aim to finish the morning's calls to allow time before lunch to discuss what has happened so far. In the review of the calls, the field sales manager should adopt the following sequence:

1   First give full recognition for successes and strengths in work.
2   Take each call in turn and reconstruct it together. He will have his memory, the manager will have his evaluation form notes.
3   Question him, where relevant, to reveal weaknesses in technique.
4   If the salesman's perception of what happened differs from the manager's significantly, reconstruct his actions to him, quoting his own words, describe his actions, and likewise the customer's words and reactions.

Remember: the purpose of this reconstruction is not to foment an argument with the salesman. If this happens the manager as a trainer has failed.

It is vital that the salesman *accepts* the manager's assessment as *fair* and *accurate.* This acceptance will be greater by the salesman if he sees the manager as a mirror reflecting his performance back to him.

In conducting field sales training, the manager should never convey, in either his words or attitude, that he is trying to pick holes, catch the salesman out, or check on him.

It is worth repeating that training cannot succeed in an atmosphere of censorship.

The aim of the field sales manager is that, together with the salesman, both arrive at an agreed way(s) of developing the salesman's abilities so that he (and the manager and the company and the customer) will be even more successful in the future.

Summarise the salesman's training needs. In the light of this review of the calls carried out and analysed, the field sales manager should summarise what has been discussed and agreed as follows:

Call evaluation form

Before/after training

Date . . . .

Salesman . . . .

Customer . . . .

Selling activity	Yes	No	Comments
1 *Pre-call planning* Did he have specific objective for call?			
Did he prepare information?			
Did he have a call plan?			
Did he have sales aids prepared and checked?			
2 *Opening interview* Did he gain attention?			
Did he explore needs?			
Did he get customer talking?			
About his needs?			
3 *Sales presentation* Did he use visual aids?			
Did he match benefits to customer needs?			
Did he anticipate objections?			
Did he get customer involved?			
Did he use simple language?			
4 *Handling objections* Did he recognise objections?			
Did he handle them satisfactorily?			
Did the customer accept the answers?			
5 *Close* Did he ask test questions?			
Did he recognise buying signals?			
Did he ask customer for order?			
Did customer order?			

Figure 11.3 Call evaluation form

1 Give recognition for the strengths and successes shown.
2 Define carefully and precisely the agreed weaknesses the field sales manager will attempt to correct during later training calls.
3 None of us finds the revelation of shortcomings palatable, however skilfully shown, so discuss the progress he has made in areas of weakness dealt with in previous field training visits.
4 Thank him for his help in analysing his morning's work.
5 Never select more than two training objectives. Stick to one whenever possible.

At the end of this summary the plan for the afternoon's calls should be agreed and the training techniques that will be used to correct the weaknesses, e.g. coaching, role playing, demonstration by example, practice and analysis.

As a spur to the salesman's motivation to want to improve his selling performance and as a visual means of seeing it take place the manager can use a simple chart as shown in Figure 11.4. Taking the sales calls carried out so far and the results obtained from them, these can be plotted as a graph using a red pencil. When the training has been completed and the results are being measured, a second graph can be plotted in blue and then the line compared with the first one. Hopefully it will indicate in an interesting way the progress that has been made. In training, as in so many other communications, a picture is often worth a thousand words.

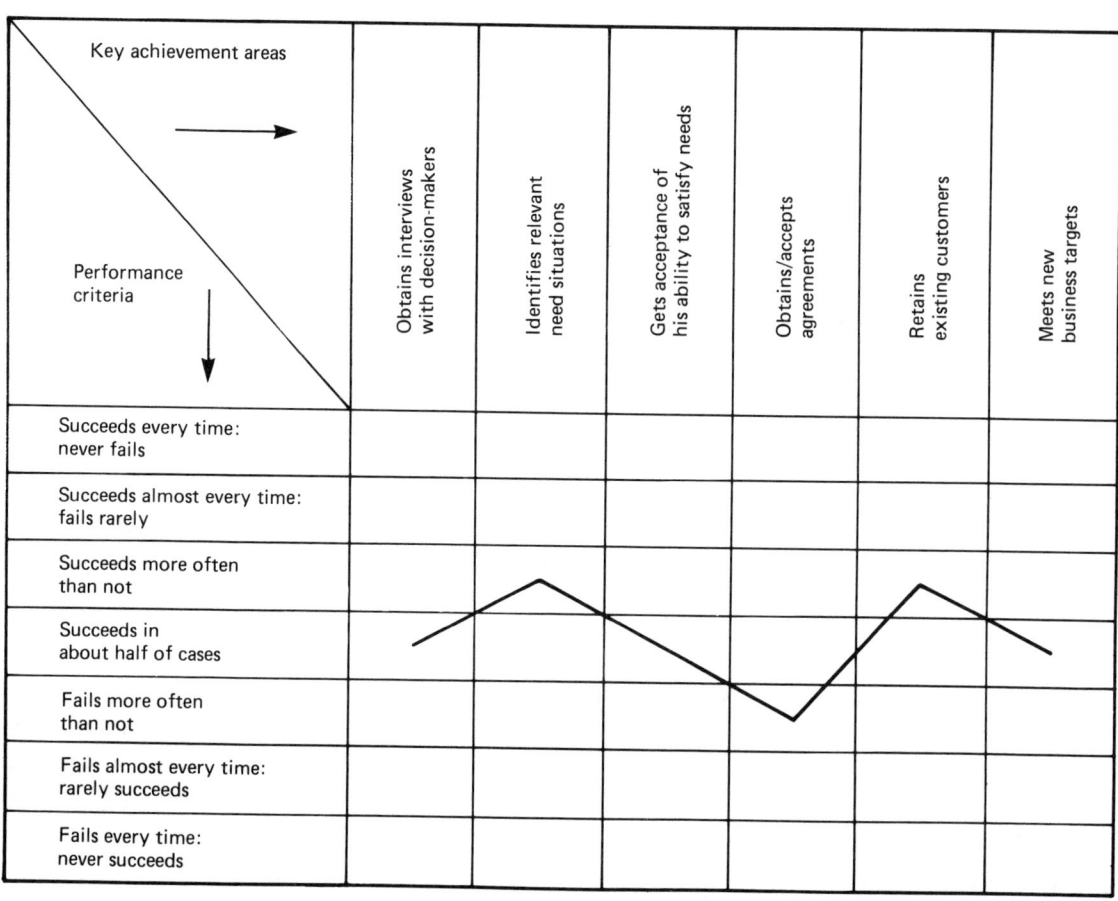

Figure 11.4 Sales performance evaluation grid

Day one: Afternoon

Training objective: to develop a selling skill(s)

After a morning's calls and the subsequent analysis, some managers will decide that the afternoon should be spent in a hotel room conducting a series of role-playing exercises. Such a decision must be weighed up very carefully. If it is done badly, the loss of morale and self-confidence can outweigh any good.

In the majority of situations, the best development takes place in front of the customer where there are no second or third prizes for a good attempt. The salesman either obtains the call objective or he fails.

It is important to remember that when the field sales manager is using the ten steps technique (see Chapter 8) the call rate will drop. More time will be taken to plan each call and in reviewing it afterwards. The results of a drop in call rate may not be significant in overall terms for the week or the month, but to the salesman it might cause anxiety. The manager should anticipate and deal with it, stressing the benefits that this will bring in better results and more effective calls later.

Day one: Evening

Training objective: review improvements achieved

The day has been one of performance, analysis, and then training and development for both the salesman and the manager.

At the end of day one the manager should remember that day two is going to be spent by him in measuring how successful his training has been. So it is important to summarise what has been done so far so that the salesman goes home in a positive frame of mind and is motivated to maintain this improvement:

1 Recapitulate the results achieved in day one.
2 Stress the points on which the salesman should concentrate on the next day and in future.
3 Thank him for his efforts and help.

Day two

Training objective: measuring the results of training

Day two of the suggested two-day field sales training visit to a salesman should be spent observing and measuring how calls are conducted following training. Use a call evaluation form, as shown in Figure 11.3, to record what happens on each call so that comparisons can be made with those completed for calls made on customers during the morning of day one before any training was given. At the end of day two these completed forms provide an overall picture of performance, comparison, and hopefully, of progress. Review these with the salesman. Re-emphasise the points on which he has improved and those on which he should concentrate between then and the manager's next visit.

Use a salesman performance appraisal form as a means of summarising the final discussion with the salesman and for agreeing what actions are needed and when and in which area of sales performance.

Complete the rating for each section of the form after agreement has been reached with the salesman. Remember there will be ample fact upon which agreement can be founded. Before parting company, the manager should tell the salesman approximately when he plans to accompany him again. He should also agree upon a date by which the salesman will have completed and returned a copy of a salesman performance appraisal, indicating his personal assessment of his own selling skills on a given day or number of days, just prior to the next field training visit.

Action planning checklist

	Answers	Action and timing
1 Is there a programme of regular and systematic training for experienced salesmen in the field?		
2 Does the company have an organised programme and structure for the field training of experienced salesmen?		
3 Does field sales management spend sufficient time with each salesman, when field training him, to effect real improvement in selling performance?		
4 Have field sales management been trained to train experienced salesmen in the field?		
5 Do the field sales management use a salesman performance appraisal system as a means of identifying selling performance and to determine training needs?		

12: How to Conduct Successful Sales Training Meetings

The field sales manager is judged by the *combined* sales produced by his team. In previous chapters you have learned how to carry the individual training and development of *new* and *experienced* sales personnel. During the course of any one year, your individual appraisals will reveal that your sales team have some common training needs or weaknesses. These may range from company/competitor product knowledge, a selling technique such as closing or an aspect of their work organisation. When this occurs, you have two choices. You can plan and carry out a programme of training on an individual basis for each of your salesmen. This will take time and you may feel that immediate action is needed to correct this common weakness. A more speedy and effective solution might be to bring the sales team together and conduct a group training meeting. In most companies employing large and small sales forces, local training meetings held on a regular basis are commonplace. It has been estimated that more than ten thousand internal sales meetings are held in the British Isles alone every week.

Assuming that a salesman works about two hundred days a year, if a field sales manager holds a one-day sales training meeting for ten people including himself, he incurs costs which may well run into thousands of pounds. There is the administration, hotel costs (if held at such a venue) plus the nine days' selling opportunities deliberately sacrificed. Some years ago, a computer manufacturer reckoned that the opportunity cost of a two-day sales meeting exceeded £150 000. For all these reasons it might be imagined that managers would make sure that there was always a justifiable purpose for holding a sales meeting. That each one was carefully prepared; professionally conducted and, above all, that it achieved specific, measurable results. Yet far too many meetings fail because they lack specific objectives, have been given scant if any preparation and little discernable improvement takes place afterwards. Or, as one long suffering salesman succinctly, if cynically put it; 'one bad meeting begets another, and another, and another . . . . . You can always trace the seeds of chaos back to the confused mind that called the first one.'

Objectives of sales training meetings

The objectives should be:

1 To carry out group training and development.
2 To inform and get feedback from the sales force.
3 To provide a meeting place and forum for your salesmen.
4 To stimulate and, if necessary, rekindle salesmen's enthusiasm and motivation.

All these must be inspired by the main objective which is the effective development of the sales force to achieve planned sales targets. In Chapter 4 reference was made to customers eroding selling skill. The particular value of the sales training meeting lies in the opportunity it affords to combat the eroding effects on selling technique and morale of being geographically dispersed with infrequent occasions to meet each other.

For these reasons each meeting must be carefully planned and conducted with great skill so that measurable results are achieved by everyone when they return to their sales territories.

Ingredients of a successful meeting

There are *five* ingredients required to ensure that the company, the field sales manager and the salesmen get practical value from sales training meetings:

1 The objective is a *specific* and *limited* one. The temptation to cover a number of topics is immense. Resist it and your head office colleagues who want to make an input. One subject, explored in depth is worth more than three or four dealt with superficially.
2 There is *a plan* for achieving it. Know how you are going to start the meeting, involve everyone, how you are going to develop knowledge or skill, how you are going to end.
3 The person conducting the meeting must *prepare himself,* the *place* and the *people* who are attending it. To conduct a half or one-day training meeting probably necessitates setting aside at least one day well beforehand to prepare yourself. So many meetings fail because so few people give themselves sufficient time to prepare.
4 The meeting is conducted *professionally.* This is much more likely to happen if point 3 is borne in mind.
5 *Specific follow-up actions* are established to measure whether the meeting's objective has been achieved. The acid test of a successful meeting is what those who attend it are able to do better, or differently afterwards not whether everyone enjoyed it.

Set a specific objective

It is all too easy to call a sales meeting to review the monthly sales figures, to give out routine information, to praise or blame the salesmen for the results. It is less defensible to have one simply because it is a week, a month or even a year since you held the last one.

A *specific objective* must be set that is relevant to the current commercial situation; moreover one that is important to *all* who will be present and not to just one or two. It helps to define the meeting objective by using the three criteria listed in Chapter 8 'Field training methods and techniques':

1 What should those attending be able to *do* as a result of attending the meeting.
2 The *conditions* under which they should be able to do it.
3 The *standards of performance* they must achieve to be able to do it.

Examples of objectives derived from recent appraisals might be expressed as follows:

e.g. *To improve the call rate:*

> To increase the number of effective selling calls from five to seven per day by better call planning by a specified date (an effective call defined as one wherein the salesman meets and has the opportunity to obtain a buying decision from a person in the customer's company who has the *need*, the *authority* to place an order and the *money* to pay for it).

e.g. *To improve the number of closing opportunities:*

> To increase the number of proposals submitted from six to ten per week by improving the techniques for qualifying prospects by a specified date.

Spelling out objectives precisely means that everyone knows what the training meeting is trying to achieve. It also forces the manager calling the meeting to have satisfied himself that this objective is *correct, relevant* and one upon which all will agree. This implies that he has arrived at such an objective by analysing the sales figures and the *combined* and recent on-the-job salesman performance appraisals carried out and discussed with each person attending the meeting.

Frequency of meetings

It is sensible to plan the dates and broad objectives of sales training meetings at least six, even twelve months ahead. Dates are then in everyone's diary and a planned programme of development can be achieved. Otherwise it is difficult to ensure that the whole sales team can attend or because they cannot, meetings are postponed. The normal frequency for sales training meetings will vary depending upon the size and spread of the sales force and the nature of the business. A monthly frequency is normal for this type of meeting.

What should be prepared?

There are six parts that should be prepared:

1 Theme and meeting agenda
2 Location and training room
3 The audience
4 The activities
5 Training aids
6 The chairmanship

THEME AND AGENDA

Both should be thought about and planned ahead of the meeting. Ideally one main subject should be chosen around which to develop a *theme* for the meeting and to ensure coherence. A theme focuses the mind and provides a discipline. For example, the theme for a meeting concentrating on the benefits of planning sales activities, might be 'Get Ready, Fire, take Aim!!!' Another dealing with merchandising techniques, 'Feathering the nest'.

Everyone attending the meeting should have a copy of the *agenda*. It provides a structure which helps to avoid trying to cover too many things or giving the wrong emphasis to matters of little importance. The agenda should be short, giving the starting and finishing times. It should be designed for variety, to maintain a brisk pace and to always end on a high note. If there are routine matters of administration or credit control that have to be dealt with, they should be put first before moving on to the main theme and interest of the meeting. Items raised under 'any other business' are frequently taken at the end, are time consuming and often ruin an otherwise good meeting. Deal with any other business subjects first. Better still, circulate the draft agenda to your salesmen well ahead of the meeting asking for any comments or suggestions. This should eliminate the need for AOB.

LOCATION AND TRAINING ROOM

Whilst some companies hold meetings at their company or branch offices, this is often neither convenient nor desirable. The dangers of distraction are too great. There are a wide variety of hotels and conference centres available with good meeting facilities and equipment. They provide a spacious environment and surroundings that can be conducive to a productive meeting.

Training Room

The room in which your meeting and collective training is to be held must be large enough to seat all attending, preferably at tables so that notes can be taken. The objectives and how you plan to achieve them determine the room layout. Classroom style for a session devoted mainly to a lecture by one person; a round table or open square for discussions or an open forum. Everyone must be seated within the speaker's vision and be able to see clearly any written material displayed on a flip chart or screen.

Lighting should be good, but not dazzle the audience. If a film is to be shown, there must be accessible power points, the room must have blacking-out facilities, be long enough for projection and the ceiling high enough to accommodate the projection screen when fully extended. These points are so obvious but too often overlooked. Figure 12.1 gives a checklist of things to remember.

THE AUDIENCE

Size

It is important to get the right number of people to match the objectives of the meeting and how you plan to conduct it. For example, if you are going to carry out a series of role-playing exercises, record and play them back on closed circuit television and discuss, each role-play will take from forty-five minutes to one hour. If you have more than six to eight salesmen, the role plays will drag on and become very boring.

Jobs and status

Make sure that there is sufficient in common to allow role playing, questions and subjects to be discussed freely and without reservations. Some older or senior salesmen may not like their shortcomings to be shown up in front of junior or much younger colleagues. If anyone from another area, or from head office is invited, their presence could hinder the chances of a successful meeting. As a general rule, for a training session the person running the meeting should never have anyone senior to himself present. If he does, the participants are unlikely to want to expose their failings by exercises or role playing. Training should always take place in an atmosphere *free from any form of censorship and amongst people of equal status*.

Any guest should be introduced to the audience at the start and the reason why he is

General facilities	Room	Delegate Requirements	Agenda	Chairman
Location Overnight accommodation Eating arrangements Charging and invoicing arrangements Telephones Cloakrooms Lavatories Message handling	Size Layout Chairs Tables Lighting Ventilation Electrical sockets Window blinds Ashtrays Water and glasses Microphone	Notepaper Binders Pencils Erasers Name badges *Refreshments* Morning coffee Lunch Afternoon tea	Items requested Theme Finalised Circulated *Audience* Selected Notified Briefed Visitors	Sales manager

PROGRAMME

Session	Content	Method	Visual aids	Hand-outs	Timing	Speaker
Example: to increase knowledge of how to plan selling calls on prospective customers	• How people buy • call objectives • customer research • call structure	Lecture/discussion	Overhead projector with prepared slides	Session notes • sales manual • call planning section checklists and guideline notes	90 minutes	Field sales trainer
Example: to improve identifying information needed and for closing such calls	Résumé of techniques: practice using real life customer situations	Film Role-playing	16 mm projector and screen	Notes on major techniques with examples	Film – 30 minutes Discussion – 30 minutes Role-playing – 60 minutes	Sales manager

Notes: Notify salesmen to bring one category A prospective customer details
Ask training department to lay on pre-view of best training films on call planning from Rank and Video Arts to be screened at least four weeks before meeting

Theme for training session to head the advance agenda: 'Get Ready, Fire, Take Aim!!!'

Figure 12.1 Sales meeting planning form

attending. Likewise new salesmen should be welcomed immediately so that they can feel relaxed among new colleagues.

Knowledge and intelligence

Beware of mixing young, numerate graduate salesmen with others who are not, when there is a correlation between the work to be done and intelligence. For example, salesmen whose formal education finished when they left school, might find it difficult to understand sales forecasting techniques or financial ratios.

THE ACTIVITIES

It is vital to give a lot of thought to maintaining attention and interest throughout the meeting so that the learning that takes place can be turned into action later. People learn far more by trial and error constructively analysed than by just sitting and listening. Dependent on the purpose of the meeting (to impart some new information, or to develop or improve a technique in which your sales team has a collective weakness) one or a combination of the following training methods can be used.

- Lectures
- Demonstrations
- Discussions
- Role-playing
- Individual projects/presentation
- Brainstorming
- Quizzes
- Film
- Video tape recorder
- Tape record
- Slides

Let us examine some of these methods in greater detail.

Demonstrations

The value
This technique can be used for a group and of course for one person in the field. It can be very effective, but does not develop skills when used on its own. Demonstration helps learning particularly when a live illustration is needed especially before role-playing, for example how to handle a specific sales objection.
 It can also be used:

- As a method for establishing your own competence as a trainer (to dispel the unspoken objection, 'I wonder if he can do it himself?')
- To convince people when doubt is expressed that a recommended method works.
- To help remember.
- To add to past or future learning.
- To relieve boredom.
- To set a standard.

Caution

The skill of the demonstrator must be high. But if done too well so that it dazzles every observer rather than trains, it can demoralise a new or slow salesman. If a demonstration goes wrong, the credibility of the demonstrator and the subject can be lost. This can happen when you demonstrate the wrong and then the right way to do something. There is also the danger of trying to demonstrate *too much* in one go.

Running a demonstration

When running a demonstration, either at a sales training meeting or any other situation, it should follow the basic principles of training:

1 *Tell* those watching what you are going to do in outline, then in detail, broken into stages if needed (the length of each stage will depend on the experience of those being trained).
2 *Show* them – actually do the demonstration (or part of it if the total operation is complex).
3 Allow those watching to *practise.*
4 *Observe, guide, correct* and *coach* where necessary.
5 *Move* to the next stage, linking it to the completed stages.
6 At the end, *revise* the demonstration and *summarise* the total exercise.

Discussions

Value

Group discussions can be an effective way of training and introduce a change from the normal sales meeting.

1 The topic can be structured to illustrate the points most relevant to the group and the training needs.
2 The pace can be set to enable common understanding
3 Feedback from the group guides the training given, and indicates whether it is being effective.
4 Disagreements or particular problems are identified and resolved.
5 The experience of the whole group benefits the whole group (including the trainer).
6 Participation and involvement lead to commitment.
7 Everyone 'learns' without being 'taught'.

Effective discussion leading requires a high degree of skill, and involves very careful planning and preparation by the trainer.

The trainer in effect plays the role of a group member with the added privilege of co-ordinating the views of its other members. His role is to stimulate thought and discussion by the group, to listen very carefully to all that is being said and to ensure a common understanding by the group of the points under discussion. He needs to be *challenging* but *patient, provocative* but not *argumentative,* and has the responsibility of achieving his training objectives by obtaining agreement within the group.

Preparation

In preparing a training session based on discussion you should structure the preparation as follows:

1 *Decide your objectives*
   ● What is the objective of the session?
   ● How does it relate to other training given?
   ● What level of understanding is required?

2 *Analyse the topic*
- Decide on a logical sequence.

3 *Subdivide the sequence*
- Divide the logical sequence using appropriate headings.
- Assess the ground to be covered under each heading.

4 *Plan your introduction*
- What is the knowledge and experience of the group?
- How can their past experience be related to the topic?
- What is the best way to introduce the logical sequence and the headings?

5 *Prepare your discussion*
- Write out your headings
- Anticipate discussion
- Prepare suitable questions to stimulate discussions
- Prepare your own views and notes for guidance
- Decide how particular points can be illustrated
- Arrange a group seating plan which will ensure free discussion
- Prepare headings on the flip chart

Leading and handling the discussion

Always use a carefully planned introduction. Keep it as brief as possible, but ensure that you give a general outline of the whole topic to be discussed.

Relate the topic to the group's past experience

End the introduction with a general question to start discussion under the first heading on your flip chart. When you have asked your first question *wait* for discussion to start. Do not be afraid of silence.

At all times you should ensure that everyone understands the discussion. Welcome disagreement as an opportunity to clarify everyone's perception of the topic.

In every discussion group, you will find two opposites, the 'discussion hoggers' and the silent ones, with the rest of the people in between. Both extremes are vital to the success of the discussion, but need careful handling.

The discussion hoggers. They are invaluable in getting discussion started, but often talk for too long. If you 'shut them up' you will risk losing their contributions, but if you allow them too long the discussion can become a dialogue with most of the group bored and disinterested.

You must use their contributions, but by passing additional questions to other members you can involve everyone in the group and divert the discussion when necessary.

There will be times when you will meet a 'hogger' who just will not allow his colleagues to contribute. Under these circumstances several gentle techniques can help:

1 Make a friendly joke at his expense
2 Ask another member of the group what he thinks of the hogger and his views
3 Ask him to write down but not to voice his views on the 'next three questions'.

But do it all gently and with a smile!

The silent ones. Remember:

- silence need not be agreement,
- silence need not be understanding.

Encourage contributions from them by:

1 Giving encouraging looks in their direction
2 Referring to their particular experience e.g. '. . . . . I know that you have met this problem recently'.
3 Asking them a direct question.
4 Giving them something to do, eg '. . . could you work out the number of working days in the year for us?'

Be careful, however, not to exert pressure on silent members. They may be shy, less experienced or less articulate than their colleagues. Lead but don't push.

The rest of the group. Most group members are between these extremes. Obtain everyone's participation by the use of directed questions, the use of general questions 'facially' expressed to one particular member and by obtaining the involvement of each in commenting on views already expressed.

Controlling the discussion
It is important for you as the discussion leader to ensure:
1 That you understand each contribution.
2 That the rest of the group understands it.
3 That the discussion relates to the headings and divisions of the topic.
4 That you always summarise each contribution and write it under the right heading.
5 That you summarise the whole of the discussion under each heading.

Questions
The value of the discussions depends on:

1 How you introduce and summarise each aspect.
2 *How you ask questions and the type of questions you ask.*
3 How well you succeed in making each contributor feel that his points were valuable.

You should *avoid* making statements and then asking for an opinion from the group. You should avoid asking questions which only require a 'yes' or 'no' answer.

Neither of these approaches will stimulate your group to think or to understand. Instead, you should ask open-ended questions which demand thought and require a considered reply. Open-ended questions start with: What? – Where? – Why? – Who? – When? – or How?

If answers are vague or unclear, or if you doubt whether either the contributor or the group really understand the point, explore it further by asking: 'Perhaps you could illustrate your point with an example. . . . .'

In obtaining clarification and understanding, maintain in all your questions an open-minded approach so that each member and the whole group (including yourself) 'arrive' at the right conclusion and do not feel 'driven' to it.

It is useful to relate each contribution to previous ones and thereby create a structure which builds on past experience.

Using pauses and silence
In asking open-ended questions, you are provoking thought.

It is very important to allow time for this thought – no particular length of time, but just as long as it takes for one member to open the discussion. It is very tempting to start talking yourself if silence lasts more than a few seconds – don't!

The pressure which you feel to speak is equally strong on the group and it is very rare for the first contribution to take more than a minute to come forward. Wait for it to come – use pauses and silence to allow thought by the whole group (including yourself). Your discussions will be better for it. The group will quickly realise that they are working with you and are not being 'taught'.

Summarising

After each point is made by the group, it is important for you to ensure that it is understood by all. It is useful to repeat the point in your own words'. . . what has just been said is . . .' This technique not only helps to clarify the point, but ensures understanding.

Try to relate it to other points made, but beware of changing contributions to fit your own training purposes. It can be very easy and tempting to do this – particularly with difficult points – but the secret of successful training is to build confidence and trust.

Blatant misuse of your position as trainer and discussion leader will destroy both, so summarise fairly, objectively and without the use of 'literal translation' to suit your trainers perspective. The basis of good summarising is your own ability to *listen* to what is being said, to *remember* what has been said and to *say it again* on behalf of the group.

The timing of your summaries is important and allows you to structure the whole discussion. You can use summaries to move on to the next heading if time is pressing, or you can delay summaries to allow a particularly valuable discussion to continue. You should base your timing on the needs of the group and not on the needs of the timetable.

Summary

As the discussion leader, you are there to train the group by serving it:

1   Prepare thoroughly.
2   Ask the right kind of questions.
3   Listen and check.
4   Balance the discussion by ensuring participation by each member of the group.
5   Summarise at intervals and at the end, but only when the point is understood.
6   At all times be patient, unhurried and balanced yourself – *you are a member of the group.*
7   If appropriate use your summary as a basis for follow-up action in the field.

Role-playing

The most effective approach to developing selling skill is to involve people by trying to help them find solutions to their own real life selling problems. Using the 'live ammunition' of actual customer situations brings a double benefit. For the salesman it is seen as a deliberate means of solving his problems or to open up a new opportunity. For you as field sales manager what is prepared and role-played as a dress rehearsal in the group training can be followed up and assessed in real life.

Salesman preparation

Ask each salesman to bring one or at most two, customer situations to the meeting. The material may consist of the customer records and notes made on the last call. You and the salesmen may have chosen the customers or prospects when you last accompanied each one.

At the meeting ask each salesman to take one of the customer situations he has brought with him and write down on a piece of paper all the information available about the customer,

e.g. ● type of business
     ● what is bought/not bought
     ● buyer – type of person – attitude to salesman, salesman's products
     ● when the last call was made

- what happened
- what was the outcome of the call
- if he did not buy, what were reasons given for not buying, etc.

Give each salesman two pieces of carbon paper so that the customer information is produced in triplicate. This enables those role-playing the customer, the salesman and you the trainer to have a copy each.

Once these customer situations have been written down, pair off the salesmen at the meeting. Ensure that those of similar age and selling experience work together. In each pair the salesman whose customer situation is used as the basis for the role-play will play the part of the customer; his colleague will be given a copy so that he can play the part of the salesman selling to the customer. Give both time to prepare themselves for their respective roles. Stress to the salesman playing the customer role that he should think about the proposition as though he was really making the buying decision. This will increase the salesman's understanding and perception of the customer's needs. His colleague playing the part of the salesman is quite likely to bring a fresh and possibly an innovative selling approach to his role playing. So both gain from this role play.

The role play

If possible try and carry out the role-playing in a separate room from the training room. Record and play back the selling using closed-circuit television and video tape or sound recorder. See Figure 12.2. This arrangement enhances the realism of the setting for the selling yet enables the observers unseen by the role players to watch the whole interview and make notes on the good and bad points. To help the salesman role playing ask each of the observers to evaluate a specific part of the sales interview, using the call Evaluation Format on page 137. Before the role play begins it helps the observers' evaluation if first the salesman playing the customer tells them in the absence of the salesman role player, what the customer situation is and how he proposes to handle the meeting with the salesman. The salesman does likewise with his colleague who is role playing the part of the customer absent as would happen in real life. At the completion of each role play, first ask the seller how he felt he had carried out the selling, what was good about it what was not? Then ask the customer for his views. Next ask each observer salesman to evaluate the part of the interview he had been asked to watch, feeding back the good points first then those that were bad and why he thought so.

Finally, you as the manager should summarise each role play emphasising the good points brought out and in particular any others that the observing salesmen missed; comment constructively on any weak points and how they can be dealt with. Make sure that the salesman whose customer situation was role played summarises what he has learned and will be using when he next sells to this customer.

Role playing value is:
- For training in selling skills.
- To enable group learning through observations analysis and practice.
- For trying out new skills, techniques, or ideas.
- For correcting bad habits and encouraging good ones.
- For practising skills shown in demonstration.

The advantages

1 Gets close to reality without the risks of practising skills on customers.
2 Is the only successful way of changing habits outside the work situation.
3 Helps to convert knowledge and attitude changes into skills.
4 Enables trainer to *develop* the *learning* started by other methods and *to link off-job with on-job training*.

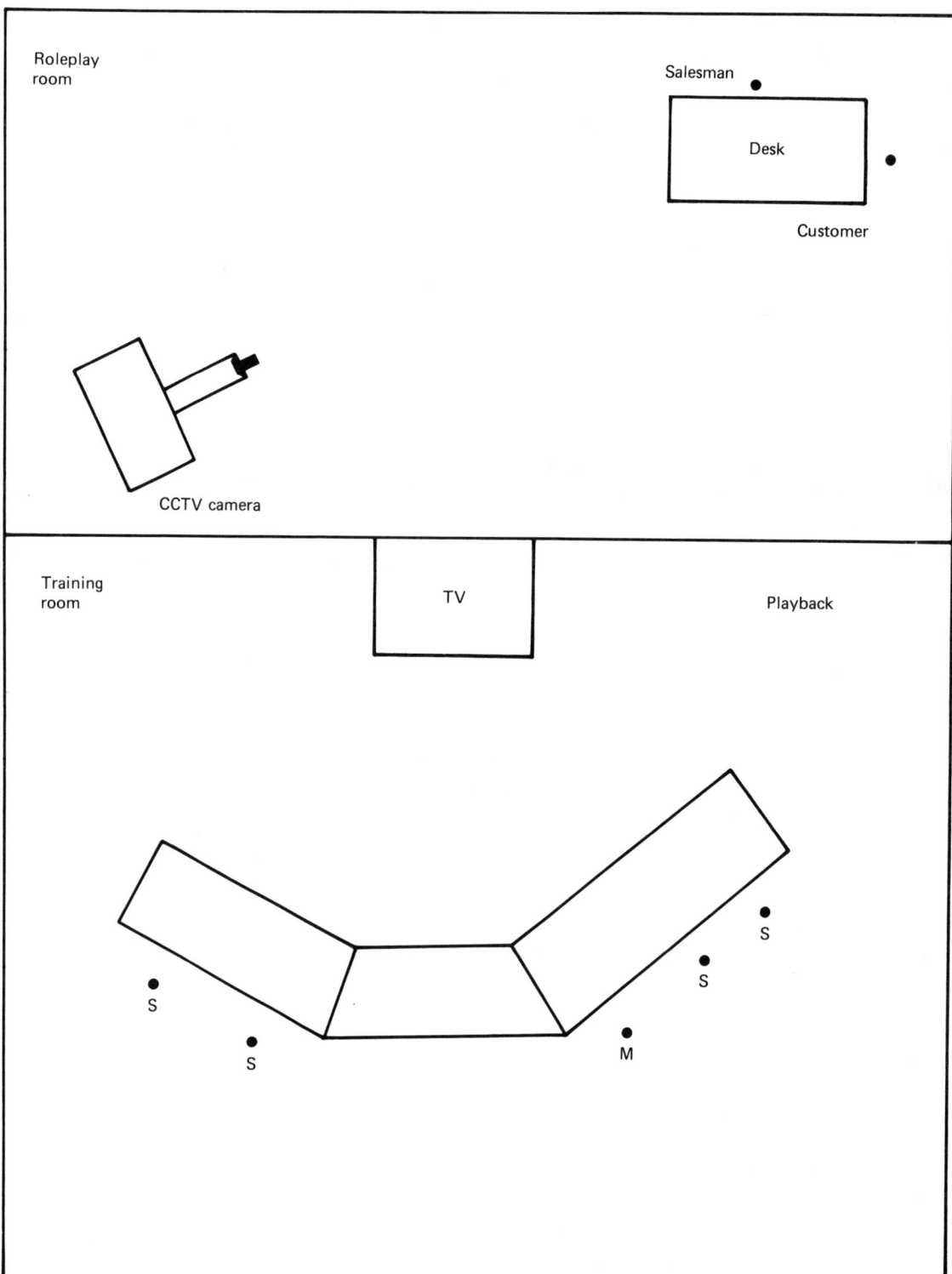

Figure 12.2 Room layout for role playing

5   Gives the manager feedback as to the effectiveness of previous training.

Caution
1   Results can mislead the manager (some trainees become 'professional' role players).
2   Requires time and resources.
3   Needs a high degree of skill, patience and understanding.
4   Avoid acting situations.
5   Keep participants of similar age and experience together.
6   Avoid direct observation by other managers.
7   Some people can be badly affected by role playing situations.

Brainstorming

Another effective teaching approach is 'brainstorming' real-life selling problems experienced in trying to expand major customers or worthwhile prospects.

On every sales territory there are usually two or three major prospects who, for one reason or another, the territory salesman has so far not converted into a buyer. Converting them can often be speeded up by using the sales meeting as a workshop during which new approaches can be researched, or better and more convincing answers to objections can be discovered.

In one case a major soap manufacturer held a series of brainstorming sales meetings in small groups made up of the area manager, his six salesmen and an outside expert as chairman. A major prospect in each salesman's territory was brainstormed on the following basis:

1   Each salesman gave his colleagues a factual background of his prospect, e.g. name, position, type of contacts, type of customer, size of business and competitor currently holding the business. He then described the calls he had made on the prospect, the objectives of each call, who was seen, how he opened each sales interview and the reactions, how he presented his case and what happened, objections raised and how he answered them, how he had tried to close the call(s) and the answers received to his request for business. These details were written up on a flip chart to aid call analysis and discussion.

2   Armed with this knowledge about the prospect, the chairman then invited the team to think about the following factors:
●   The amount of information known about the prospect and his needs.
●   The methods of approaching the prospect so far used and alternatives to them.
●   Developing a new creative strategy and approach for this prospect.
Throughout these discussions four guidelines were kept in mind by everyone and underlined by the chairman when necessary:
●   Judgement was suspended – all ideas were considered without criticism.
●   There should be no restraint – the wilder the ideas the better. After all none so far attempted had produced results.
●   Quantity – the more ideas the better.
●   Cross fertilise – one idea helped to combine and improve the ideas of others.

3   At the end of the free-ranging discussion during which ideas and approaches were recorded on flip charts, the chairman then drew together those that could be used to develop a practical customer strategy.

From these meetings a number of lessons were learned, two of which stood out: salesmen were making calls on prospects and trying to sell their products from the word go, instead of collecting a sufficient body of knowledge of the customer's needs. The second lesson was that salesmen saw each call as a self-contained one rather than as part of a coherent customer strategy. This led to one-shot approaches where the call objectives were either wrong or over ambitious.

Incidentally following these sessions in one area four of the six customer strategies developed produced new business where none had been hitherto enjoyed.

Another approach used by a clearing bank is similar to that already described. Here, however, the managers who are responsible for new business development plan a real prospect call and then role-play the meeting using closed circuit television to review the call. These rehearsals have had a marked effect on the subsequent results obtained.

TRAINING AIDS

Visual aids, skilfully introduced and used in a talk or presentation, can often convey an idea or piece of information more effectively than a verbal description.

Too often managers visualise what is better said and say what would be more effective if visualised. So how do you decide what to do about visualising your presentation? Ask yourself *four* questions once you have compiled the information for your sales training meeting:

1   *Do I need any visual aids at all?*
2   *What visuals are necessary?*
3   *What important points in my presentation would be better understood by a visual/picture than by words?*
4   *What picture or memory do I want the audience to take away?*

The answer to question 4 helps you to choose the one *key* visual aid for your presentation. It could be the only one you need.

Characteristics of good visuals

They must:

1   *Be readable (or understandable) from furthest point in room.*
    Always, before your presentation, go to the furthest point in the room from the screen on to which your visual is to be shown, or the table on which a model or exhibit is to appear and check that what you plan to visualise can be both *seen* and *understood* by everyone, Make allowances for the fact that, from the back of a chair, the average adult's body when sitting extends to about another two feet above it.
        If your visuals are *not* of uniform lettering/word size, then you must carry out this check for each one you propose showing.
2   *Produce impact immediately*
    A visual is used to gain or to regain attention which may have wandered during your introductory remarks. Sketches, pictures or diagrams, have more impact than words.
3   *Have as few words and as big as possible*
    Avoid too much detail on one visual aid. Keep information to about *four* lines maximum. Letters when projected should be three inches high. Keep numerical information to minimum. People do not remember figures easily.
4   *Be easy to read and simple to understand*
    Use short words, none at an angle or uʍop ǝpᴉsdn.

Visual aids: do's and don'ts

DO	*DON'T*
1. Keep visuals simple.	1. Use a visual aid if you have any doubts about it.
2. Check visuals are readable from furthest point.	2. Visualise what can just as well be said.
3. Use as few words as possible.	3. Use 'Visual verbal'.
4. Use key words; key phrases.	4. Show a visual until needed.
5. Design visuals to relate directly to words being spoken.	5. Take your audience through your slide presentation too quickly; some may want to make notes.
6. Use visuals to complement a presentation.	6. Be afraid of silence.
7. Use correct colours in visuals.	7. Compete with your visual aids; let them speak for you.
8. Use pictures/sketches rather than words.	8. Leave visual/slide/projector on when you have dealt with the point your visual was shown to make.
9. Use charts rather than figures.	9. Show a visual without first introducing/explaining it.
10. Rehearse using your visuals.	10. Switch overhead projector on and off without reason.
11. Let your visuals speak for themselves.	11. Mask your visuals by standing in your audience's line of sight.
12. I need any visuals at all?	12. Talk to your visual aids.

Summary

Rules for using visual aids

1. Identify the parts of your presentation where a visual aid will help communicate your ideas better than just relying on words.
2. Select your aids – too few rather than too many.
3. Ask yourself: – do they do what I want to communicate?
   - are they as simple as possible?
   - could they be misunderstood?
   - will they distract the audience?
   - could the machinery break down?
   - will they work?
4. Prepare your visual aids thoroughly, no matter how simple; very basic things, such as pencilling outlines or a check-list of headings on to a flip chart before your presentation can turn an ordinary talk into a very professional one.
5. Keep them hidden until required.
6. Introduce the visual aid before showing it.
7. Let your visuals speak for themselves. Give the audience time to read or study them before proceeding.
8. Any comments made by you whilst showing a visual should be brief, concise explanations of the content.
9. Check to ensure everyone understands. There is no point in developing the subject if some of your audience are confused.

10 When your visual has done its job, remove it from sight; otherwise it will compete for your attention of the next point you want to make.

Visual aids can help you to improve the chances of your presentation being successful. After all if you speak you are only using one of the five senses through which we send and receive messages. Whereas if you show a picture to your audience you are appealing to a second means by which we send and receive messages – sight.

They can attract attention that has wandered, add a picture to your words, hold or regain attention, simplify what was complex, challenge with a memorable vision and summarise.

So a variety of aids can help to stimulate and hold attention better, for example, a training film, slides, models and charts. Professionally prepared material is now becoming very expensive, but there are always some talented impoverished students at art colleges who for a few pounds will produce some arresting visual aids. The lasting impact of a picture is still worth many thousands of all too soon forgotten words.

THE IMPORTANCE OF SKILLED CHAIRMANSHIP

Having set a specific objective and prepared a structure to achieve it, success depends heavily on the quality of the chairman. He must adhere to the timetable, because this gives a sense of pace and variety which is essential to maintain interest.

Each stage of the meeting should be summarised so that everyone understands what has so far been agreed and achieved and what progress is being made. The maximum amount of participation must be encouraged because those at the meeting want more from it than just the satisfaction of being able to say: 'It was a good meeting – I spoke'. They need to leave with answers to specific sales problems. See Figure 12.3, which is a helpful check list for chairmen.

CONCLUSION

Sales meetings are becoming much more costly and for this reason alone many failures cannot be accepted. In the eyes of the sales people, the management is often only as good as the last meeting. If it was a bad one there is a problem – getting them to come to another one. All meetings should therefore have:

- A *specific* and *relevant objective.*
- Prior *preparation* of *subject, salesmen* and *venue.*
- A good *opening* to rivet everyone's attention.
- A good *middle,* using visuals, discussions and practice to maintain interest and to aid the learning process.
- A good *ending* in which there is collective and individual commitment to specific actions afterwards.
- An assurance that these *actions* will be *followed up* and any progress charted.

1. Was I friendly? Did I 'break the ice'?
2. Did I act as chairman, not as lecturer?
3. Did I hold back my own opinion?
4. Was I free from prejudice and fair to all?
5. Was I patient?
6. Was I enthusiastic?
7. Did my questions provoke thought?
8. Did I introduce the meeting topic properly?
9. Did I word the problem properly?
10. Did I avoid 'yes/no' questions?
11. Did I withdraw into a guiding, not a driving position?
12. Did I watch the trend and interject stimulating remarks at the right time?
13. Did I clarify and/or illustrate all important points?
14. Did I refer questions back to the group instead of answering them myself?
15. Did I discourage useless and dangerous discussion?
16. Did I tactfully draw out shy or reserved members?
17. Did I handle over-talkative members tactfully?
18. Did I keep the discussion to the point?
19. Did I secure individual participation?
20. Did I acknowledge every relevant suggestion?
21. Did I keep the discussion moving towards a proper conclusion?
22. Did I keep the meeting open until all the facts were in?
23. Did I offer a new topic when the old one was exhausted?
24. Did I summarise?
25. Was my work on the overhead projector etc. fast and clear?
26. Did the discussion cover as much ground as was practicable?

Figure 12.3 Checklist for chairmen

REHEARSING IS ESSENTIAL

Frank de Angeli, Vice Chairman of Johnson & Johnson International and formerly Managing Director of the UK company, gives his views on the importance of sales meetings: 'Any manager calling a meeting should pay those who are to attend it the courtesy of not only preparing it thoroughly but also of rehearsing it beforehand before a group of his management colleagues'.

How many of the managers who are holding the thousands of sales meetings that are taking place every week have even attempted to rehearse what they are going to do and how they are going to do it?

Action planning checklist

	Answers	Action and timing
1 Are sales training meetings held regularly to develop knowledge and skill?		
2 How well planned are they? Do you set aside at least one day to prepare them?		
3 What measurable objectives do you set for them?		
4 What follow-up on the job do you plan?		
5 What motivational value do your sales meetings have?		

13:

Motivation through Training

Getting planned sales objectives achieved through the efforts of the salesman implies that the salesman will want to achieve such objectives because there will be some benefits which will satisfy his needs.

The field sales manager can only harness the efforts of the salesman by understanding the inner drives, needs, and hungers that move him to action, showing him how these can be satisfied, and then motivating him to want and welcome training as a means of achieving his objectives and those of the company.

Motivation consists of understanding the internal emotions and needs of human beings and providing inducements which will cause them to employ their full abilities in their work.

The individual needs of salesmen will differ in nature and scale, but broadly speaking the opportunity to meet and satisfy the most urgent of them will have been the principal motivation why one man joins a particular organisation in preference to another.

In nearly every study of human behaviour the need to find *job satisfaction* has been identified as the prime motivator. Maslow described it as ''self actualisation' and Herzberg listed several needs under this general heading, e.g. the work itself, and the needs for recognition, achievement, advancement, and responsibility. Two factors common to all these needs are that, first they are intrinsic to the job itself, and second, they are to a very large extent capable of being satisfied through the development of skill.

1 *Work itself.* Since most people have to work for a living there is a basic desire to find work that will satisfy and fulfil. In an increasingly educated society this desire will increase and the attraction of selling will depend upon whether it is seen to meet this need. It can do through training.

2 *Recognition.* Everyone has a need to be recognised for the social worth of his job and respected for the competence with which he carries it out. In an increasingly competitive society the choice presented to the customer and the similarity between the products, services, and supply lines of competing marketing organisations, enhance the importance

of the salesman. Training can help him to become a vital part of the company's marketing effort and to be singled out for recognition.

3   *Achievement.* Selling is a dynamic activity in which to achieve new sales targets, open up new business and enlarge existing customers' business. Training will help a man to do this more thoroughly, more creatively, and more often.

4   *Advancement.* Not everyone wants advancement nor the responsibilities of management, but for those who do training will help to develop capabilities and test them.

5   *Responsibility.* The great majority of salespeople, whilst not wanting to become managers, nevertheless want to advance in terms of responsibility within the work they do. They want training to equip them to shoulder wider selling responsibilities, and for this work to be recognised in status and rewarded financially. It is an indictment of many companies that they have offered the tinsel in the shape of bigger cars, grand-sounding titles and more money, but not *real* enlarged responsibilities. Training competent staff to take on more responsible sales work rewards the staff, the customers, and not least, the company. (The controlled experiment in job enrichment carried out in one division of ICI is worthy of study. It was discussed in an article, 'Job Enrichment Pays Off', by W. J. Paul, K. B. Robertson and F. Herzberg, *Harvard Business Review,* March/April 1969.)

The link between the salesman and the realisation of one or all of these needs is the field sales manager; the catalyst is his ability to train and develop each person to change as required and to be happy in work and at work.

How can the manager motivate through training? Surprisingly, the answer is a simple one: *'sell – don't tell!'*

If we examine the steps in the process of selling to a customer and training a salesman, we find they are exactly parallel. In fact, selling and the techniques of sales training are synonymous:

	Trainee salesman		*Customer*
1	Needs training but does not know he needs it.	1	Has needs but is not aware of them.
2	Realises he needs some training.	2	Realises he has those needs.
3	Is motivated by the trainer to want training.	3	Is motivated by the salesman to want to buy.
4	Listens and learns.	4	Places an order.
5	Develops new skills and succeeds.	5	Confirms the benefits he has bought from the salesman.
6	Welcomes and asks for more training.	6	Becomes a regular customer.

This approach to training is equally important at every stage of the training operation. Here the catalytic effect of the manager is illustrated:

	Salesman		*Field sales manager*
1	Needs training but does not know he needs it.	1	Helps salesman to see the need for himself: 'Let's look at this problem together.'
2	Realises he needs training.	2	Helps the salesman to see the benefits of training in his job.
3	Is motivated by the trainer to want training.	3	Stresses the particular benefits to the salesman, relating benefits to salesman's own personal needs.
4	Listens and learns.	4	Presents all his training from the sales-

	man's point of view: 'How does this relate to your problem?'
5 Develops new skills and succeeds.	5 Builds 'Success' into all his training methods and carries it forward into the job and to the satisfaction of the salesman's needs.
6 Welcomes and asks for more training.	6 Works with the salesman to identify the next stage and how it will help with the salesman's new problems.

The field sales manager needs to ask himself the following questions to marry the needs of the company, the salesman and of himself together.

1 What are the needs of the salesman?
2 What does the company expect of the salesman and what standards should be set for selling skills and work organisation?
3 What standards are the salesmen achieving as a group and as individuals?
4 What is the gap between standards set and actual performance as a group and as individuals?
5 How can I get the salesmen to identify for themselves that training is needed?
   - What are the needs/benefits to them in their job?
   - What are the needs/benefits important to each of them as individuals?
6 What training is required to close the gap between performance and standards?
7 How can I present training on the job so that it is seen as helping the salesmen to solve their problems and satisfy their needs?
8 How can I continuously evaluate my training activities so that the training provided continues to meet the changing needs?

The action planning checklist shown will help the field sales manager find the answers to these questions and put the principles of motivation into action.

TRAINING SALESPEOPLE TO TRAIN

Among the wider responsibilities which salespeople can be trained to shoulder and with considerable motivational implications, is training them to train other salespeople.

Many companies, large and small, have found a reservoir of talent for teaching and training among their salespeople. If this is spotted and such salespeople are given thorough training to train, using the methods and techniques presented in this book, the field sales manager has increased his ability to develop his salespeople.

Salespeople who become sales trainers should be rewarded for this additional responsibility with a salary increase and possibly different grade of company car.

The advantages of training salespeople to train are that it provides the field sales manager with a trained resource, when he recruits more than one new salesman and needs help with initial field training, and enables him to assess the management capabilities of one or more of his salespeople without first having to promote them into a management position. It will also motivate the salespeople who want wider responsibilities and yet do not want to become managers.

HOW TO LINK MOTIVATION AND TRAINING WITH CONTROL

The common thread in how to motivate salespeople through training has so far been by 'selling it'. But motivating, like all sales management skills, must be used to pilot the sales force towards planned objectives. This means that motivation and training must help maintain *control,* a word many managers dislike and few readily associate with motivating salespeople.

The word tends to give off the smell of autocratic government; of conformity and stifling of initiative. It is rather like the words 'incomes policy'! There are no votes in it, yet we all try and have one in our personal lives if only to ensure enough money is left to take us away for an annual holiday.

The best control mechanism anyone can have is the deep and abiding satisfaction derived from the job he does. In order to get this satisfaction and control his own performance the salesman needs to know more than what his goals are. He must be able to measure how well he has done by two sets of standards: his own personal standards, and those standards which can also be seen, recognised, and accepted by others, e.g. his colleagues, his field sales manager, his company. Far too often salespeople find they are measured by standards which are not always compatible with these two yardsticks, e.g. sales volume is only a motivating standard if the salesman reaches or exceeds it. Yet in the process of failing to meet sales volume, he may have excelled in every factor within his control and that of his sales manager.

The right controls used correctly are the key to motivation and are essential to effective training and management. The right controls are also those which are derived from consultation and agreement with the salespeople. His agreement and commitment to them become his controls; and self-control means stronger motivation.

Action planning checklist

	Answers	Action and timing
1 What are the needs of each salesman?		
2 What does the company expect of each salesman?		
3 What standards should be set for selling skills and work organisation?		
4 What standards are the salesmen achieving as a group?		
5 What standards is each salesman achieving?		
6 What is the gap between standards set and the actual performance as a group?		
7 What is the gap between the standards set and the actual performance of each salesman?		
8 How can I get each salesman to identify for himself that training is needed?		
9 What are the needs/benefits to each man in his sales job?		
10 What are the needs/benefits to each man as an individual?		
11 What training is required to close the gap?		
12 How can I present training on the job so that it is seen as helping the salesmen to solve their problems and satisfy their needs?		
13 How can I continuously evaluate my training activities so that the training provided continues to meet the changing needs of the company and those of each of my salesmen?		

14: *Training to Train the Field Sales Manager*

Having read this book from cover to cover or dipped into chapters here and there, some field sales managers will have learnt sufficient to apply all of it; some will learn by discussing its contents with colleagues and then applying the skills effectively; some will have that rare gift of learning by thinking things out for themselves and then applying the techniques; but for a great many learning comes from *doing* it. So the question will be asked by many, many managers: How can I be trained to train my salesmen on-the-job? Some managers may be responsible for just one salesman in a small business while others may be one of several in a large company with a sales force of over 100 people.

EXTERNAL COURSES

For the manager of one or two salesmen who is probably doing other jobs as well, possibly even the managing director of his own business, he can attend an external course. The number of such courses, however, is vast, so he must select a programme which will meet his needs. Here are some guidelines to help make that selection:

1 *Define the training objective.* To help clarify what the field sales manager's personal training needs are he should write down four questions and answer them (see Figure 14.1).
     ● What do I need to know and understand?
     ● What must I be able to do?
     ● What are the circumstances in which I must be able to do it?
     ● What standards must I reach to be able to do it?
   This personal training-needs analysis enables the manager to assess the objectives and content of any course much more effectively. Above all, it pinpoints what a training objective is for him: *what he is able to do at the end of the course.*
2 *Send for information about training courses for the field sales manager.* Write or telephone course organisers, tell them what your training needs are, and ask them if they have a

Questions	Answers/knowledge	Skills
1 What do I need to know and understand?		
2 What must I be able to do?		
3 What are the circumstances in which I must be able to do it?		
4 What standards must I reach to be able to do it?		

Figure 14.1 Personal training needs – field sales manager's analysis

programme to meet them. If they do, it is obviously necessary to check the dates when the programme runs. Much more important, check the quality of the programme. Three pieces of information will help to answer this question:

   (a) Who actually runs the programme? What are their qualifications as salesmen, field sales managers and above all as trained trainers?
   (b) Which companies by name have used the course regularly?
   (c) Ask for the names and telephone numbers of at least three people in positions similar to your own who have attended the course and to whom you can speak about it.

4 *Choose a suitable programme and attend it.*

5 *Decide what follow-up action is necessary.* The most important decisions to be made at the end of a training programme are what actions must be taken to ensure that the investment of time and money yields a productive return. Obviously, applying the techniques learnt is the simple answer. But there are other actions that should be considered.

   (a) Keep in touch with the other members of the course you attended. Some may manage field sales operations similar to yours, so the exchange of experiences in applying the lessons of the programme can be invaluable. Others may be in fields far removed such as selling banking services, pharmaceuticals or defence equipment. Again their contrasting experiences will be well worth exchanging.
   (b) Compile a reading list *and then read the books on it.* The course director probably suggested a reading list for you. If he did, well and good; but if not compile one that will help you to understand more deeply what you have so far learned and how to do it better. A suggested reading list is included at the end of this book.
   (c) Evaluate your effectiveness as a trainer. If you already have a systematic salesman

appraisal system in your company then you have a tool with which to assess the improvements your training produces after the course. If not, set one up so that comparisons can be made. You will, of course, be able to measure the differences in sales volume, but not in the quality that went into achieving the increase. Once your sales performance appraisal system is installed, however, you have a means of assessing the progress of the sales force month by month as a group and as individuals. Evaluating training is very difficult because of the influence of external factors outside the control of the salesman, but it is worthwhile making some attempt to do so. For the sales force as a group, evaluation can be made by comparing budgeted and actual sales before and after training, as shown in Figure 14.2. For the individual salesman, evaluation can be by comparing budget and actual sales before and after training and by plotting an additional piece of information: field visits to the salesman before and after the training course you attended (see Figure 14.3).

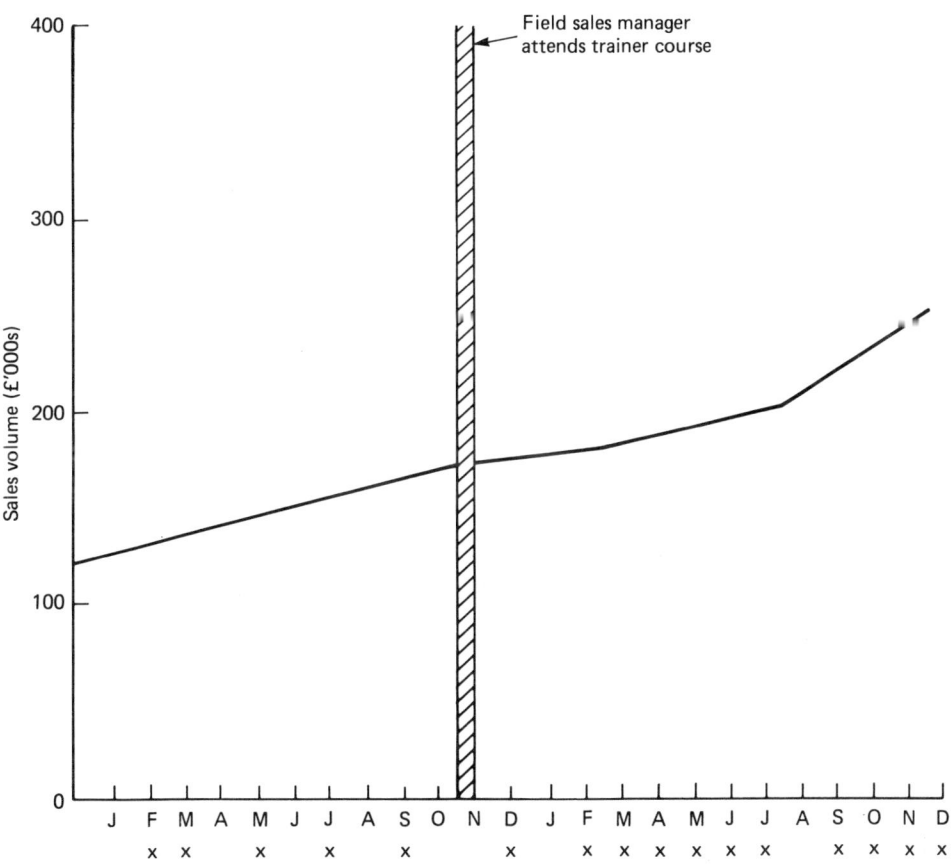

Figure 14.2 Comparison of sales volume before and after training

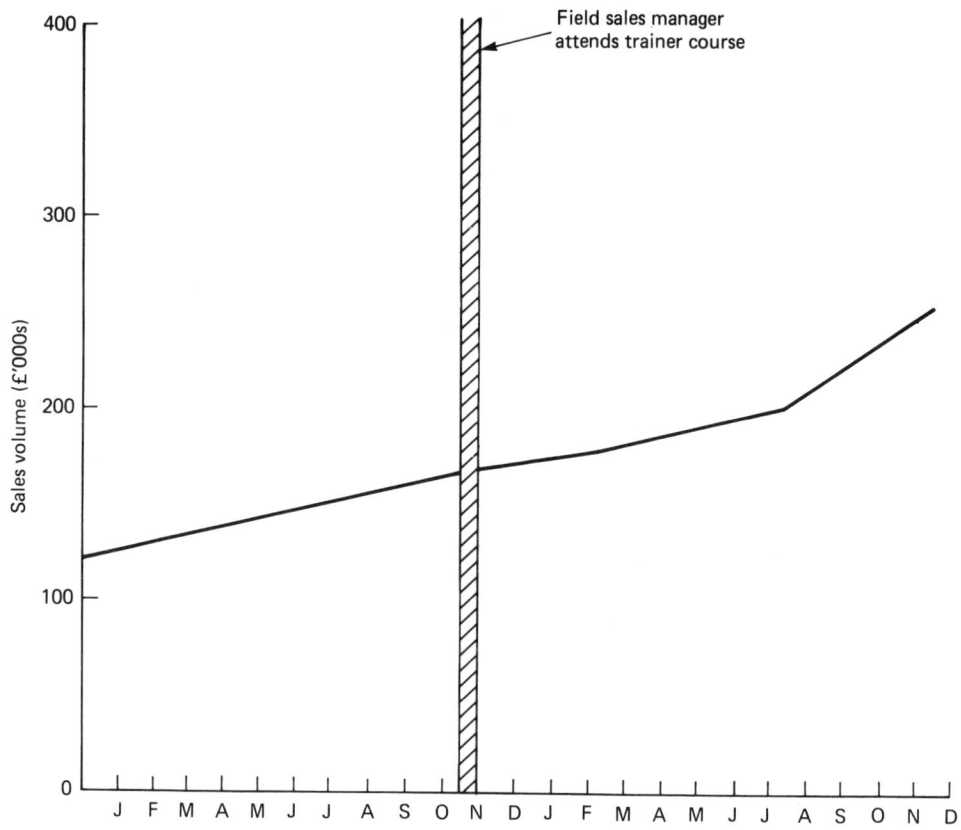

Figure 14.3 Comparison of performance before and after training in relation to field sales manager's field training visits

INDIVIDUAL TUITION

As an alternative to attending a 'train the sales trainer' programme, a field sales manager could arrange to have a programme of private tuition, spread over a period of weeks, from an acknowledged expert whose qualifications, business experience and training are appropriate. Again, the approach to the analysis of personal training needs is as described, but the planning of the tuition will require a lot of care and thought. Some ideas about the sequence for this tuition can be derived from the training programme illustrated in Figure 14.4.

On a straight cost comparison, individual tuition will be more expensive than attending an all-comers general course. On the other hand, some of the benefits outweigh the additional cost. For instance, one day a week may be much less disruptive to a small business than being absent for a whole week; much more time can be given to the study of a specific aspect of field training as it applies 'to my sales force' to 'this particular rather dyed-in-the-wool salesman'; the most urgent priorities can be dealt with; techniques examined on one day's tuition and then applied can be discussed on a subsequent tuition period and further coaching given.

Timetable	Notes
Day one	
09.00 Welcome and introduction	Course opened by senior manager to stress importance company attaches to training Course members give their backgrounds − if unknown − to one another
09.15 Importance of training	Stress that company's and individual's objectives cannot be achieved unless people are trained to achieve them
10.30 Coffee	
10.45 Motivation and the role of training	Develop the concept of training meeting the individual needs of salesmen
12.30 Lunch	Long lunch break to enable work to continue into late evening when necessary
14.15 The training role of the field sales manager	If the manager can't train he can't manage. This is the prime job function to be underlined
15.30 Tea	
15.45 Identification of training needs	Managers carry out training-needs analysis based on their salesman's job description(s)
17.00 Break	
17.15 Salesman performance appraisals	Introduce the system for developing selling skill on the job and as a tool for use by manager and salesman together
18.15 Case study	Managers work in pairs developing a salesman performance appraisal system
Day two	
09.00 Group Reports	Managers present their appraisal systems
10.30 Coffee	
10.45 Aims of field training	Introduce six objectives to be achieved, benefits of structured sales interviews, how sales interviews should be conducted
11.30 Break	
11.35 Aims of field training	
12.30 Lunch	
14.15 Principles of learning and communication	Managers take part in communication experiments to discover difficulties of communication
15.00 Film: 'More than Words'	Illustrates in simple cartoon form how barriers to communication can be overcome and learning improved
15.30 Tea	
15.45 Field training methods and techniques	The advantages and limitations of each method are analysed
16.45 Break	
17.00 Initial on-the-job training of a new salesman	The importance of this training in setting lifelong habits stressed the length of time to give to it analysed in light of manager's experience
18.30 Briefing for role-playing	Managers prepare to role play field training of new salesmen

Figure 14.4 Field sales manager training programme

Timetable		Notes
Day three		
09.00	Role playing	Managers role play in pairs field training of new salesman; recorded on closed-circuit television; played back and evaluated
10.30	Coffee	
10.45	Role playing	
12.30	Lunch	
14.15	Role playing	
15.30	Tea	
15.45	Role playing	
17.00	Evaluation of exercise	Each manager sums up what has been learned about training new salesmen on the job and compares previous methods
Day four		
09.00	On-the-job training of experienced salesmen	Importance of training and developing *all* salesmen on a planned and regular basis
10.30	Coffee	
10.45	Film: 'Training Salesmen on the Job'	Reinforces techniques for training experienced salesmen
11.15	Briefing for role playing	Managers prepare to role play field training of experienced salesmen
11.45	Role playing	Managers role play in pairs field training of experienced salesmen; recorded on closed-circuit television, played back and evaluated
12.30	Lunch	
14.00	Role playing	
15.30	Tea	
15.45	Role playing	
18.00	Evaluation of exercise	Each manager sums up what has been learned about training experienced salesmen on the job and compares with previous methods
Day five		
09.00	Preparation of action plans	Managers prepare action plans based on course stating what they propose to do about the on-going training of their salesmen on returning to work
10.30	Coffee	
10.45	Presentation of action plans	Each manager presents his proposed action plans for the on-going training of his new and experienced salesmen. Action plans to include training objectives to be achieved; methods and standards and timings.
12.00	Final discussions and Course Summary	Restate course objectives, deal with final questions
12.20	Lunch	Course ends

Figure 14.4 Field sales manager training programme — *concluded*

HOW TO STRUCTURE A COMPANY TRAINING PROGRAMME

A great number of fast-moving consumer, industrial and service companies employ more than one field sales manager and so can either organise through their sales training manager or commission a specialist consultant to design and conduct an in-company course. The length of such a course will obviously depend upon the content and the numbers attending it. Here are some guidelines on how a 'train the field sales manager as a trainer' course might be constructed.

Course objectives

Dependent upon the nature and scale of the field sales manager's field-training responsibilities and duties, the course objectives might include all the following ones:

At the completion of the programme, the managers will be able to:
1 Understand the importance of training as a key management task and skill
2 Plan the individual training of new and experienced salesmen
3 Develop their skill to analyse individual training needs
4 Develop their skills to conduct on-the-job training for new and experienced salesmen

Content of programme

Based upon these course objectives the material covered would include the following elements:

1 *The training role of the field sales manager.* The prime importance of training is the cornerstone of the field sales manager's job and its motivational implications should be recognised. If a manager can't train he can't manage to achieve the results he needs through his salespeople.
2 *Motivation and sales training.* So many managers think of motivation in terms of financial incentive schemes, instead of as a vehicle for helping salespeople to achieve not only financial rewards, but their deeper longer-term needs to enjoy their work and find it satisfying.
3 *Principles of learning.* This is not an area about which managers usually have a great deal of knowledge. It will help them to learn on the course, apart from enlarging their understanding of the learning process for their salesmen.
4 *Salesman performance appraisal.* The relationship between appraisal, training and individual development. How and when to carry out appraisals and the involvement of the salesman in them, their contents and their outcome.
5 *Setting training objectives.* How to analyse training needs and define training objectives is a weak area for most managers. It is vital that it should be strong, otherwise an enormous amount of time and energy can be expended on the wrong priorities.
6 *On-the-job training methods and techniques.* How to train and develop new and experienced salespeople, of which managers will usually have a preponderance of the latter.
7 *Measurement of training effectiveness.* Managers need to relate all training to the standards necessary to achieve their planned objectives. Therefore training and its effectiveness must be evaluated.

Method of training

The programme must be carefully designed to apportion sufficient time for the maximum amount of participation and discussion of each subject. While lectures are the main means of giving knowledge, the greatest time should be given to skills development. This time will be allocated to group studies, individual analyses, and role playing with some means of feedback – ideally closed-circuit television.

Role playing.

A leaf can be taken from the chapter on role playing and the value of live ammunition. Each manager attending the course should be asked to document the details of two real-life customers or prospects in one or more of his salesmen's territories. Ideally these should be ones that he will be dealing with on his return from the course. These can then be used as material for two role-playing situations in both of which he will be involved as the customer. A method of role playing is:

1 Objective: to develop skill in field training a new salesman.
   Managers form into working groups of three; one to play the part of the customer, one to play the part of a new salesman and the third manager plays the part of the field sales manager accompanying the new salesman on an initial field training visit. The manager, in the role of salesman/demonstrator will use the customer case material provided by the manager playing the part of the customer. A selling call will then be prepared, with the manager helping the new salesman to do this; the call is then role played and the analysis of the call afterwards – both being recorded on closed-circuit television. Each role-play is then played back and evaluated, the observing managers using an evaluation form to structure their thoughts on the 'kerbside conference', technique as shown in Figure 14.5.
2 Objective: to develop skill in training experienced salesmen using the ten steps technique.
   In this role playing, the same procedure is followed, but the manager carrying out the field training will coach by using the ten steps technique. To help evaluate their colleague's performance a specially constructed evaluation form should be used such as shown in Figure 14:6.'

Length and numbers on course

To cover the material and develop skills so that they can be applied on the job at the end of the course means that numbers must be limited. It is best if there is an even number and that it does not exceed six and nine is an absolute maximum. Figure 14:4 shows a course spread over a period of five working days.

CONCLUSION

These are some of the methods through which the field sales manager can develop his skill in carrying out his prime and most productive job – *training his salesmen on the job*.

Failure to equip himself to provide sound, professional and regular training is to surrender control. He works more often than not with average men; he needs above-average results. This cannot be achieved by sterile appeals to pride or by inspirational pep-talks alone.

The results he needs can rarely be achieved without field training and the development of a soundly-based job structure on which salespeople can grow, work and sell. The field sales manager must create the difference he needs.

'Kerbside' Conference carried out by . . . .

Place a tick in the column that represents most closely the standard you feel was achieved by the Manager. Make notes in the space provided to explain you markings.

Activity	Well done	Unsatisfactory in parts	Comments
1 Did he praise the salesman for skills well used?			
2 Did he question the salesman to reveal faults? Or Did he have to tell the salesman what his faults were?			
3 Did he get the salesman to accept what his faults were?			
4 Did he instruct/ demonstrate/show how faults could be put right?			
5 Did he tell the salesman what follow-up action was required? Did he say when he would check improvements?			
6 Did he conclude by encouraging the salesman?			

Figure 14.5 'Kerbside' conference technique evaluation form

171

Role playing carried out by . . . . as manager . . . . as salesman

Steps	Evaluation				Comments
	S	AA	BA	U	
1 Analysis of record card					
2 Call Plan and Call Preparation					
3 Agreement of salesman					
4 Definition of manager's role during the call					
5 Sales call: Opening					
Presentation					
Handling objections					
Closing					
6 'Kerbside conference' Did he praise the salesman?					
Did he question him?					
Did the manager have to identify faults?					
If so, did he do so?					
Did he get agreement and acceptance of faults by the salesman?					
Did the manager show/ instruct the salesman how to rectify faults?					
Did the manager state what follow-up action was required?					
Was the salesman given encouragement?					
7 Was the record card completed accurately?					
8 Were specific objectives set for the next call?					
9 Were objectives set recorded by the salesman and by the manager?					
10 Was a date set to check improvement?					

Grading: S = satisfactory   AA = above average   BA = below average   U = unsatisfactory

Figure 14.6 Ten steps in field sales training evaluation form

Action planning checklist

	Answers	Action and timing
1 Does the company regard the prime job of field sales management as training? If not, write down what the job of the field sales manager is.		
2 Have the field sales management's training needs in terms of knowledge, skills and attitudes been analysed? (See Figure 14.1).		
3 Does the company have a specifically-designed programme to train and develop the field sales management as trainers?		
4 If not, have arrangements been made for the field sales management to be trained by external courses/tuition?		
5 What controls have been established to measure the effectiveness of the programme of training to equip the field sales management as trainers?		

Further reading

The following books have been chosen because they deal in a practical way with the important subjects related to the job the field sales manager carries out – recruitment and selection, selling and sales training, motivation and management.

Marketing

Philip Kotler *Marketing Management,* Prentice-Hall, 1980
M. T. Wilson *The Management of Marketing,* Gower, 1980

Management

P. Drucker *Managing for Results,* Heinemann, 1964 Pan, 1967
P. Drucker *The Effective Executive,* Heinemann, 1967 Pan, 1970

Sales management

J. B. J. Lidstone *How to Recruit and Select Successful Salesmen,* Gower, second edition, 1983
J. B. J. Lidstone *Motivating your Sales Force,* Gower, 1978
P. Forsyth *Running an Effective Sales Office,* second edition, Gower, 1985
M. T. Wilson *Managing a Sales Force,* second edition, Gower, 1983.

Selling

J. B. J. Lidstone *Making Effective Presentations,* Gower, 1985
J. B. J. Lidstone and *The Sales Presentation,* Gower, 1985
P. B. Kirkby

J. B. J. Lidstone	*Negotiating Profitable Sales,* Gower, 1977
A. V. Melkman	*How to Handle Major Customers Profitably,* Gower, 1979
National Training Systems/	*Creating Major Sales,* 1981
Markcting Improvements	

Sales Training

R. F. Mager	*Preparing Instructional Objectives,* Fearon, 1962
P. Forsyth (editor)	*Managing Sales and Marketing Training,* Gower, 1984

Man Management/Leadership

J. Adair	*The Skills of Leadership,* Gower, 1984
F. Herzberg	*Work and the Nature of Man,* Staples Press, 1968
N. Hamilton	*Monty, The Making of a General 1887–1942,* Hamish Hamilton, 1981

Index